THE FUNNY

About the author

Alan Bramson was born in Southport, Lancashire and brought up in Liverpool. During World War II he learned to fly at No. 1 British Flying Training School, an RAF unit located at Terrell near Dallas, Texas. There he was commissioned and gained his wings, obtaining the highest qualifying marks on the course.
Since the war Alan Bramson has been a commercial pilot, managing director of a department store in the London area and, from 1971, a self-employed aviation writer. THE FUNNY SIDE OF FLYING marks his 'coming of age' as an author since it is his 21st book. He is a regular contributor to a dozen or so aviation magazines published throughout the world and in the course of writing airtest reports he has flown some 240 different types of aircraft, from single-seat racers to a four-engine passenger jet.
For ten years, until his retirement in 1983, Alan Bramson was Chairman of the Panel of Examiners which tests civil flying instructors on behalf of the UK aviation authorities. He is a Fellow of the Royal Aeronautical Society and a Liveryman of the Guild of Air Pilots and Air Navigators. His other interests include engineering, photography and playing jazz on the piano.

By the same author

Be a Better Pilot
Make Better Landings
The Book of Flight Tests
Master Airman
Principles of Flight (audio-visual)

With Neville Birch

The Tiger Moth Story
Captains and Kings
A Guide to Aircraft Ownership
Flying the Vor
Radio Navigation for Pilots
Flight Briefing for Pilots Vols 1 to 8
Flight Briefing for Microlight Pilots
The Aerad Navigation Trainer

THE FUNNY SIDE OF FLYING

by

Alan Bramson F.R.Ae.S.

Illustrations by Trevor Ricketts

BLANDFORD PRESS

LONDON NEW YORK SYDNEY

First published in the UK 1988 by Blandford Press
an imprint of Cassell plc
Artillery House, Artillery Row, London SW1P 1RT

Distributed in the United States by
Sterling Publishing Co., Inc.,
2 Park Avenue, New York, NY 10016

Distributed in Australia by
Capricorn Link (Australia) Pty Ltd,
PO Box 665, Lane Cove, NSW 2066

British Library Cataloguing in Publication Data
Bramson, A.E. (Allan Ellesmere)
The funny side of flying
1. Aeroplanes. Flying - Stories, anecdotes
I. Title
629.132'52

ISBN 0 7137 2087 5

Typeset by St George Typesetting, Redruth, Cornwall
Printed in Great Britain by Cox & Wyman Ltd, Reading, Berks

CONTENTS

Introduction 1

Chapter 1 The Boys in Blue 3

Chapter 2 After the War was Over 22

Chapter 3 The Airline Types 37

Chapter 4 Coping with Airports 51

Chapter 5 So you are off to the Costa Fortune 65

Chapter 6 In the Posh End of the Ship 79

Chapter 7 Overheard on the Radio 93

Chapter 8 Irish Department 106

INTRODUCTION

Aviation is one of those few activities which demand that even the amateurs must be professionals if they want to age gracefully. A pilot's attitude towards flying must be totally different to the relationship that exists between the average driver and his motoring. For example, how often do we walk around our car to check there is a wheel on each corner before starting a journey? Have you not seen cars being driven with a door partly open or a yard or two of lady's coat trapped outside so that it gently sweeps the road? Do you, an undisputed ace of the motorways, check the oil level every morning or look for water in the radiator more frequently than at yearly intervals?

Flying, on the other hand, is a serious business, entailing constant inspection of the aircraft by the pilot and regular checking of the pilot himself by other more senior examples of the breed. Airline pilots, even captains with rings of gold braid up to their armpits, must endure medical checks, instrument checks, route checks and competency checks, while flying instructors are retested every two years.

I labour all this to illustrate that flying is, for want of a better word, different. Certainly, aviation is a formal business, but it nevertheless has its own humour, much of it based upon service life (the RAF, Fleet Air Arm and Army Air Corps). However, civil aviation has inspired a number of unlikely yarns which poke fun at everyone from pilots in the air to air-traffic controllers on the ground – and that is very healthy in a serious profession.

While giving lectures in various countries, I have often

told some of the stories included in this book; but if the outraged reading public wishes to apportion blame for encouraging me, all rude letters, writs and threats should be directed to the City Livery Club of London, for this august body once invited me to give a lecture entitled 'The Funny Side of Flying'. That invitation was rash enough but their request for an encore several years later was, I would have thought, some kind of self-inflicted punishment. Perhaps the chairman had a grudge against the members. However, it was brother-in-law Michael Elias who talked me into writing this book and those who wish to compose a personal letter of complaint may have his address, provided they send me a postal order (uncrossed) to the value of £5.

Ask most folk if they know any aviation stories and they will either tell you the one about the pilot who, having done a beat-up over the local golf-course, tells his nervous passenger, 'fifty per cent of those on the ground nearly had an accident just then', to which his friend replied, 'fifty per cent of us up here just have'; or the very rude one (certainly unfit for mixed company) which ends with the wife telling her neighbour that her husband has '. . . only been up twice and he was sick on both occasions'. You may rest assured that I shall be telling neither of those.

I am indebted to the many amusing friends, alcoholic and otherwise, within and outside aviation, who over a long period have entrusted me with the following unlikely yarns. I must also thank two friends in particular for their additional, quite unrepeatable, stories. These have been removed from the text by kind permission of the editor.

AEB
London 1988

Chapter 1

THE BOYS IN BLUE

Royal Air Force Padgate, located a few miles outside the garden city of Warrington, Lancashire, was a bleak centre for 'rookies' (new recruits): a vast collection of black huts punctuated by parade-grounds and ghastly kitchens where even the flies committed suicide. World War 2 was only a few months old when I assembled at Liverpool Central Station with a number of others and made the short train journey to a new life.

As we neared the camp rain started to bucket down, the sky became darker and the wind blew. For the few weeks of my stay at Padgate the weather never changed, even though there could be blue skies with little white clouds a few miles from the camp. The experience was make or break for the young men who had joined the RAF. There was much to learn about a new social structure called 'rank'. An AC2 (aircraftman second class, known in the trade as an Erk) was the lowest example of humanity; an AC1 (aircraftman first class) little better. A leading aircraftman (LAC) was regarded with some respect, while a corporal was endowed with the first vestiges of authority.

To us youngsters, sergeants and flight sergeants seemed to enjoy powers of life and death (they could put you on a charge for having dirty buttons), but towering above all were the warrant-officers, most senior of the senior non-commissioned ranks.

It was while walking through the camp in his new, ill-fitting uniform that one of my contemporaries came face to face with a warrant-officer and, being as yet unsure of the difference between the smooth suiting of these fearsome worthies and the even smoother cloth of a commissioned officer, he threw him what passed for a salute. Now warrant-officers are akin to the Almighty but, being non-commissioned, they are certainly not entitled to be saluted.

'Have you not seen one of these before?' roared the affronted WO pointing to the large embroidered crown on his sleeve.

'Yes – sir,' replied the petrified Erk.

'Where?' demanded the WO.

'On a Bourneville cocoa tin sir,' replied the hero of the moment.

In the verbal explosion that followed, windows shook, the rain ceased momentarily and the tirade ended with the stock mode of denigration in use at the time:

'You horrible little man. How long have you been in the Royal Air Force?'

At that stage the new boy burst into tears and said, 'All bloody day.'

Most cadets learning to fly during World War 2 gained their first experience of handling the controls in Tiger Moths, little biplanes with two open cockpits. The flying instructor sat in front and his student occupied the rear seat. Until late 1943, when an electric intercom was installed, communication between the two was via a Victorian-type plumbing system, called Gosport tubes after the famous World War 1 flying school. Without some form of communications it would be difficult (but not impossible) for the instructor to teach his student.

Far and away the most demanding thing a student pilot has to learn is the landing. The aim is to fly towards the airfield in a straight, descending line so that the hardware arrives at the beginning of the runway (in those days, usually a grass one) ready to level out and touch down. Come in too high and you will probably land in the next

YOU HORRIBLE LITTLE MAN. HOW LONG HAVE YOU BEEN IN THE ROYAL AIR FORCE?
ALL BLOODY DAY.

county; approach too low and there is risk of hitting the hedge surrounding the airfield. I had this terrible habit of coming in low or 'undershooting' as we say in the trade. It defied all efforts to cure on the part of my instructor.

One day I was motoring in, engine at full chat, wheels about six feet above the meadow between me and the airfield. I was just congratulating myself on having avoided a cow that had appeared from nowhere when, to my horror, the flying instructor undid his straps and stood up in the front cockpit.

'What are you doing sir?' I enquired in some panic, to which he replied:

'I'm going to open the bloody gate to let you in.'

I never undershot again.

Later in the war, I too became a flying instructor on Tiger Moths. The work could be hazardous, although it was fun on a hot summer's day, but in the winter we died. Instructors made four or five instructional trips a day and to combat the indescribable cold we would wear a kapok inner suit like a tailored eiderdown, an outer suit of heavy canvas, a leather sheepskin-lined Irving jacket, three pairs of gloves and a flying helmet complete with goggles. Sometimes a woollen scarf, several yards long and usually knitted by a wife, girl-friend, aunt or mum, was wound around the head and face in an effort to keep out the biting cold which became progressively worse as one climbed to a safe height for the training session. To make the wearer look even more like an illustration from *The Tailor and Cutter*, his feet were clad in a pair of heavy flying boots.

For reasons I cannot remember, another instructor and I flew into an American air transport base. We parked the little Tiger Moth, all canvas and bracing wires, next to a line of Dakotas and got out of our respective cockpits attired in the manner previously described. There was a Yank standing by a Jeep and, after a double take, he stared

HEY FELLAS— THE WRIGHT BROTHERS HAVE ARRIVED!

at us in utter disbelief. Then turning to a gang of mechanics servicing the nearest Dakota, he yelled, 'Hey fellas – the Wright brothers have arrived!'

An important exercise we used to teach was instrument flying, not that there were many clocks in a Tiger Moth. To make sure the student could not see outside the aircraft (and was therefore forced to fly with sole reference to the instruments), a folding hood, rather like that of a baby's pram, could be pulled over the back cockpit. In the air it was standard practice for the instructor to ask his student what height he was flying at, what air speed and so forth: the idea being to make sure he had not fallen asleep or he was not having a crafty smoke. I remember one such training session when the conversation went like this:

Me: 'What course are you steering?'
Him: 'Two seven zero, sir.'
Me: 'What are your engine revs?'
Him: 'Nineteen-fifty, sir.'
Me: 'What is your air speed?'
Him: 'Ninety knots, sir.'
Me: 'And what is your height?'
Him: 'Five feet eight and a half in my stocking feet.'

Many of the instructors at the flying schools wanted to get on to operational flying – fighters, bombers, Coastal Command – anything to relieve the tedium of circuits and bumps (landings). There was also the risk that expensively trained flying instructors, who spent much of their time flying around the airfield, might lose the ability to navigate. So the top brass agreed to allow instructors several hours' flying each month to help keep their hand in at map reading (there was no radio in a Tiger Moth, not even a cat's whisker set). It was also something of a consolation prize for the frustrated fighter ace. Usually the time was spent flying a colleague on weekend leave to another airfield. Some strange luggage was carried in, or sometimes on Tigers during these occasions. I once saw a bicycle tied to the side of the fuselage. The aircraft landed, the passenger got out, untied four strings and then rode off.

At Shellingford, near Wantage, the chief ground instructor, one Squadron Leader Gillard, was regarded by us young flying instructors as a delightful old man (he was all of 43 at the time). He lived in the Bristol area and when time came for his annual leave, I volunteered to fly him to the nearest airfield. We crossed the spectacular Clifton suspension bridge and sailing out of the River Avon were dozens of little boats. It was a beautiful sight and I felt moved to grab the mouthpiece to my speaking tube and yell, 'Gill, look at all the boats coming out of the Avonmouth.'

Old Gillard was a little deaf and the Gosport tubes were not very effective at the best of times, but the instructor in the front cockpit of a Tiger was provided with a mirror, conveniently mounted so that he could see what his student was up to in the rear cockpit. In the mirror I could see an agitated Gillard looking left and right.

'What did you say?' enquired the chief ground instructor.

'I said look at all the boats coming out of the Avonmouth' was my reply.

'My Gawd!' came the voice from behind, 'I thought you said look at all the bolts coming out of the ailerons.'

The chief flying instructor at Shellingford was a very experienced pre-war pilot by the name of Squadron Leader Dalrymple and it was his practice to hold a flight commanders' meeting every Monday morning. One of them had a little mongrel dog which was everybody's friend on the station and was therefore allowed to attend these meetings. Possibly it did not like what was being discussed but, whatever the reason, on the day in question it decided to do a widdle on the carpet right in front of the chief flying instructor's desk.

'Dally' could be an explosive chap and the four flight commanders waited anxiously while the owner of 'Widdles' picked him up, gave him a quick wallop and threw him out of the window. They were at ground-floor level so he did not have far to fall. To everyone's astonishment, Dally got up from his desk, rushed outside and came back carrying the dog.

'There, there,' he said as he patted it. Then looking at the flight commanders, he said to the dog, 'You've got more guts than that lot. None of them would dare piss on my carpet.'

If, during World War 2, the flying instructor regarded his occupation with mixed feelings, they were of unbridled enthusiasm compared with those of the poor souls who flew the target-towing aircraft. Air gunners and fighter pilots needed shooting practice and one of the methods used was to tow a target some distance behind a tug aircraft. The target took the form of a tubular canvas drogue, rather like the arm of a man's shirt, only very much larger.

The tug aircrft used for this unhealthy activity were purpose-built with a powered winch for letting out (and pulling back in) the target which was attached to them by a long, steel cable. Most of the target-towing pilots I ever met would tell you, with some passion, that the cable was nowhere near long enough for them and that when the shooting started the safest place to be was out of the aircraft and sitting astride the drogue.

At Shellingford we had a particularly powerful species of bluebottle which was, in fact, grey but similar in design to the familiar buzzing kitchen pest. Ours were so lusty that many believed them to be powered by two engines. When grounded by bad weather, a number of us used to occupy our time by capturing one of these country flies in a matchbox. If you then opened it slightly, a leg would appear and a short length of cotton could easily be tied to it. At the other end, we stuck a cigarette paper, previously rolled around a pencil to make a miniature target drogue. Bluebottle and drogue would then be released to aviate around the room. It was a perfect working model of the real thing until the bluebottle got fed up with the exercise. Then it would stop flapping and descend head first with the drogue acting as a parachute.

Plans were laid to prepare one of our target-towing ensembles, place it in a cigarette packet and get one of the flight commanders to take it into Da!ly's office so that it could be released during one of his Monday morning meetings. Just imagine the scene. At the appropriate moment the bluebottle is let loose. It leaps out of its hanger towing the target, the chief flying instructor looks at it in utter disbelief and then explodes: 'Good God – look at that! There's a bloody bluebottle towing a drogue!' At which point the flight commanders get up, looking embarrassed, back out of the room and chorus, 'Yes sir, quite sir, why not take some leave sir. We are sure you will be all right after some rest.' At the last minute, three of them chickened out, but I do assure you the target-towing bluebottles were fact, not fiction.

After Tiger Moths, students graduated on to more advanced aircraft, many of those destined for single-engined fighters converting on to the North American AT6a or Harvard as it was known in Britain. After the little Tiger, it was a massive beast with a 550 horsepower engine. It also had two inconveniences which, at the time, we considered to be modern: radio (which is an intrusion into one's privacy) and a retractable undercarriage.

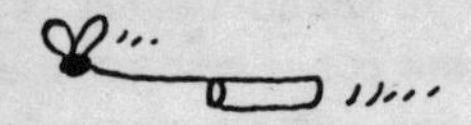

GOOD GOD-
LOOK AT THAT!
THERE'S A BLOODY
BLUEBOTTLE TOWING
A DROGUE!

The retractable undercarriage appeared on the aviation scene because aircraft were becoming faster and faster and it was no longer economical to dangle the Dunlops in the breeze, since this could materially reduce cruising speed, range and even rate of climb. However, disappearing legs brought with them that well-known aviation music-hall act, the wheels-up landing. Apart from chewing up the propeller and shock loading the engine, most of the damage caused in these incidents was confined to the pilot's ego.

My old friend Neville Birch, who got me involved in writing books, told me that, while under training, his instructor decided he would do the landing. So he did – wheels up. They climbed out of the Harvard, which was standing on the ground four feet lower than usual, and the instructor kicked it and said, 'The bastard has been trying to do that to me for months.'

To prevent such happenings, various safeguards are provided by the manufacturers. First, there are warning lights, one for each wheel; green for locked down, red for up. More dramatic is a loud warning horn which sounds off, fit to wake the dead, if the pilot pulls back the throttle below minimum power for level flight.

Obviously, the big bombers all had undercarriage warning horns during World War 2. Such an aircraft, in fact a Lancaster, arrived back from a raid over the Ruhr, a cluster of German cities where much of their armament was being made. It was four o'clock in the morning and the crew tumbled out, red-eyed and exhausted, then got aboard a small bus which drove them to the intelligence officer for debriefing. There they were given coffee and those who smoked lit up while the intelligence officer started questioning the captain. The interview went like this:

Intelligence officer: 'Well, how did you get on?'

Lancaster pilot: 'We killed one German.'

IO: 'You did *WHAT*?'

LP: 'I told you, we killed one German.'

IO: 'We send you out over Germany in a Lancaster with a twenty-thousand pound bomb load and you have the audacity to come back and tell me you killed one German?'

The Lancaster skipper was tired, he had not fully wound down from the night's activities and his temper was at breaking-point:

LP: 'Look, I am telling you we killed one German; if you don't want to know – don't ask.'

IO: 'All right, no need to blow your top. Well what makes you so bloody sure you killed one German?'

LP: 'Well, we got over the target and there was a lot of low cloud obscuring the ground. So I went down to one thousand feet and got below it.'

IO: 'That was a bit risky, wasn't it?'

LP: 'Risky it was. But my instructions were to bomb the engine works and it was the only way I could see it. I am doing my run in towards the target when, suddenly, before I was expecting it, my bomb-aimer shouted 'bombs gone'. There was a dirty great explosion, a lump of concrete the size of a tennis court came up and on it was a German working a lathe. The whole lot was right in front of the nose and the only way I could avoid flying into it was to close all four throttles. Then the undercarriage warning horn blew and the German must have thought it was the knock-off whistle because he stepped off the concrete, fell and broke his neck.'

The risks faced by the bomber boys have never been fully appreciated by the British public. They could run into dreadful weather and, through lack of modern equipment, be forced down. They could be hit by the very accurate German anti-aircraft guns. They could be shot down by enemy night fighters and, even when returning to base, a German intruder might be sitting over the airfield waiting to pounce on the tired crew as it prepared to land.

One dark, moonless night in 1943, the RAF mounted a 1,000-bomber raid on a major German city which was known to have a ring of 500 or more searchlights around its perimeter. One Lancaster bomber was imprudent enough to let itself become separated from the main force. Instantly, 500 searchlights came to life and made a gigantic cone, with the bomber at its apex. It was the prelude to every German gun in the area letting fly at that vulnerable RAF crew.

Up in the Lancaster, the intercom crackled into life as the pilot's voice announced, 'Hang on chaps – I'm going to try a new kind of evasive action.' And hang on they did; after all, was not this skipper known for his spirited flying? Would he loop the big bomber or content himself with a gentle stall turn to throw off the searchlights before the guns let fly? Instead, all he did was to close all four throttles and enter a gentle descending turn to the left.

As the Lancaster dropped in near silence, sweeping in a wide left turn, the astonished Germans followed it round and round with their searchlights. And, as the bomber sank lower and lower, so the searchlight cone became flatter and flatter until, just as the Lancaster reached 1,000 feet, all the lights went out as if controlled by a single switch. They had all unscrewed from their bases!

The big bombers were, even by modern standards, large lumps of hardware. Even bigger, and in some ways more impressive, was the Sunderland flying boat, a four-engined monster with a hull the size of a small ship. It was while being ferried to a meeting at Calshot that a well-known air marshal of mature years walked upstairs to the flight-deck (yes, the Sunderland had an upstairs long before the Boeing 747 was a squiggle on a sheet of paper) and asked if he might sit at the controls. The co-pilot vacated the right-hand seat and the skipper moved over and courteously invited the air marshal into the captain's chair.

It was some time since this very senior officer had flown, but he was managing very well until, near Calshot seaplane base, he started to let down and it soon became clear he was aiming to land at a nearby airfield instead of on the water. The young flight lieutenant in the right-hand seat gave a discreet cough and said, 'Excuse me, sir, hope you don't mind my reminding you that this is a *flying boat*, not a land plane.'

The air marshal looked startled and then spluttered, 'What – what! Yes I know, I know – only having a look at where we are holding the conference.'

At that point he made for the water and carried out a perfect arrival. They moored to a buoy, the air marshal opened the door, turned to the young flight lieutenant and said, 'Fooled you that time, my boy.' Then he stepped out and fell into the water.

So far I have confined myself to the Royal Air Force which was, in fact, formed around the air arms of the Royal Navy and the Army during the closing years of World War 1. These days, few people realise that during World War 1 our heavy bombers were operated by the Navy and that the Royal Flying Corps were part of the Army. The sailors and the 'Brown Jobs' have an attitude towards flying that is rather different to the RAF's. At one time the Navy insisted on its aircraft being all things to all men. They were festooned with equipment, much of it hanging outside – coils of rope, ladders (for boarding ship), silly little bombs that would not blow the skin off a rice pudding and marker buoys: you name it, there it dangled.

If I had any say in the matter, every pilot, Fleet Air Arm or RAF, who operated from an aircraft-carrier would be awarded an automatic VC. Think of the problems of landing on a floating runway that is much too short for a light plane, let alone such military hardware as the Seafire

FOOLED YOU
THAT TIME
MY BOY,
AAAGH!!!

(waterlogged version of the Spitfire). Just as you are about to land, the 'runway' drops ten feet or, even worse, it comes up and threatens to push the wheels through the wings.

Then there is the little matter of length. During the war it was a poor airfield that could not offer at least 1,200 yards of runway, but you were lucky to get even a quarter of that stopping distance on an aircraft-carrier, even the biggest of them. To help discourage the aircraft from running off the sharp end of the ship and disappearing into the waves below with a loud plop, a series of wires are stretched across the deck, with a large spring at each end to take the shock. The wires stand a few inches above deck level so that a strong hook, trailed below the aircraft during landing, can make contact. I believe there were five wires on wartime carriers, so there was a sporting chance of picking up one of them.

One has only to see some of the wartime films of carrier operations to realise that a deck landing was some form of controlled crash. For the benefit of non-aviating readers I feel bound to quote an old saying about aircraft-carriers that is well known to most respectable land-based pilots: 'Any landing you can walk away from is a good one.'

A young RAF pilot by name of Graham Smallwood who, like me, learned to fly at an RAF school in Texas, USA, during World War 2, came back home and was posted to an aircraft-carrier. After the war he entered the Church (I am not surprised) and recently, as Canon Smallwood of Lichfield Cathedral, he wrote a little piece for the cathedral magazine explaining the cut and thrust of carrier landings. I do not have his exact words, but they went something like this: 'There are five arrester wires stretched across the landing area of an aircraft-carrier. They are known as wire number one, wire two, wire three, wire four and, finally, the For-Christ-Sake wire.'

During the early stages of World War 2, Allied shipping

had to face the double hazard of U-boats from below the surface and German long-range aircraft from above. Although Britain managed to produce one acceptable four-engined bomber, the Shorts Stirling, a rather better one, the Halifax, and the outstanding four-engined Avro Lancaster, the mighty German industry failed to develop anything like them. The nearest contender was a pre-war four-engined airliner, called the Focke-Wulf Condor. Being a civil aircraft, it was not really strong enough for military use, but it nevertheless managed to make a serious nuisance of itself over the North Atlantic. The Condor claimed a number of Allied ships at a time when we could ill-afford to lose vital supplies.

The Condor could operate up to 1,200 miles out into the Atlantic, well outside the range of Allied fighters at the time. To combat their threat, someone proposed fitting a number of merchant ships (called Camships) with a catapult so that a Hurricane fighter could be launched when a Condor threatened the convoy. Most of the Hurricanes were old and due to be replaced, which is just as well because the first flight off the ship was often the last. The drill was that when a Condor appeared on the scene, the Hurricane would start up, the pilot would move the throttle fully forward for maximum power, and brace himself for the rocket launch (entailing a 3.5g kick in the pants), a sailor would fire the catapult and the Hurricane would climb towards the Condor, then shoot it down.

At the end of what was often a successful exercise, the pilot would then make for the nearest land or, if this were out of range, climb to a safe height, position over a ship and bale out in the hope of being picked up. Otherwise it was a long swim back to Britain. Many of the pilots were in the Fleet Air Arm, although some were from the RAF.

On the occasion I have in mind, the reader should imagine the launch scene. There has just been a deafening report and a blinding flash. Through the smoke can be seen a Hurricane disappearing in the distance and next to the Naval type who has just lighted the blue touch paper is a man in full flying kit, who taps him on the shoulder and says, 'Don't mind me; I'm only the pilot.'

DON'T MIND ME; I'M ONLY THE PILOT.

Chapter 2

AFTER THE WAR WAS OVER

The ending of a major war is an event hard to imagine unless one has experienced it at first hand. One minute factories all over the world are working three shifts and the merchandise of conflict is pouring out in floods like the waters of the Nile. All over the world, service men and women on both sides of the punch-up, in uniforms of blue, navy, khaki, grey and a few odd shades of green, live for the moment and give little thought for tomorrow; because nobody can guarantee that there is going to be a tomorrow.

The final battle is won and lost, victors and vanquished alike are stunned by the sudden return of peace, while thoughts of tomorrow take on a new attraction. Those who have lost the war are made to cease military production immediately; but to the victors, all those factories are a problem. Because if the powers that be throw the switch, skilled workers by the hundreds of thousands will overnight find themselves with nowhere to go. The pubs would be swamped and the beer would run out. So production goes on, albeit at a reduced rate, and the most unimaginable acts of State vandalism become the order of the day. I clearly remember brand-new Lancaster and Halifax bombers being flown from the factory to such airfields as Hooton Park, there to be greeted by platoons armed with oxy-acetylene torches. They would climb on to purpose-built platforms, remove the cowlings and burn through the engine mountings, thus allowing brand new Rolls-Royce Merlin and Bristol Hercules engines to hit the ground. The rest of these bombers was then reduced to scrap.

At the end of World War 2, Britain had one of the largest air forces in the world and, by way of giving the boys in light blue something to do, it was decided to exhibit our winged might to the Allies (and in some cases, near-Allies). A small grass airfield in the Home Counties was turned into a grandstand, the air attachés of friendly and neutral states were invited to attend and the Royal Air Force put on a splendid flying display which culminated in a fly-past by the mighty Avro Lincoln, an enlarged development of the very successful Lancaster. In its day, the Lincoln was an impressive piece of hardware.

The chap flying that Lincoln knew a thing or two about putting on a display. First he roared past, flat out, all four engines at full chat with the propeller tips only six feet above the grass. And about 250 pairs of eyes followed him from left to right as he shot past at more than 300 mph. He circled the field and made another run, this time with an engine stopped and its propeller feathered. And the same heads turned, a little more slowly this time, as he repeated the beat-up at about 250 mph.

A minute or so later, he came back and did it again, with only two engines running, and the eyes followed his progress from left to right as the Lincoln flew past at 190 mph. Then everyone thought, that's it – end of show; but to their utter amazement, the Lincoln reappeared with three props stopped and only one engine running. Now all this was too much for an American colonel and he was heard to say, 'OK, OK, don't tell me – so now he'll fly round on the goddam wipers.'

Soon after that, the RAF developed a passion for long-range navigation, often in converted Lancasters. There was the astonishing case of a trip that was supposed to entail flying non-stop from an RAF station in East Anglia to India but, for reasons not known to me, the navigator got his sums all wrong and they ended up flying around in circles for hours, running very short of fuel and making an emergency landing on an island off the coast of Italy. As they said in the Officers' Mess at the unfortunate chap's home base, 'The poor sod doesn't know his Madras from his Elba.'

This unfortunate young navigator came, in fact, from a family with a long RAF tradition. His father, a chap called Eaton, had been a pilot in the 1920s. There was some family money and he had bought himself a Gipsy Moth, which was the finest light plane of the period (he was known ever after as Moth Eaton). At his wedding, the fond parents gave the newly-weds a house. And Eaton's mum threw in a rather swish coffee percolator, which was something of a novelty in those days.

It had been a rather alcoholic wedding reception and after Eaton had made his speech the young bride, swaying slightly on her feet, insisted on turning to Mrs Eaton senior and announcing to all present, 'I would like to thank my new mother-in-law for my perky copulator', a statement of appreciation which received a well-merited round of applause. Of course Eaton (the 'perky' father of the navigator who lost his crew on the way to India) is by now a retired senior officer. He was with an old colleague at the RAF Club one day and his friend said, 'How's the wife, Eaton?' to which he replied, 'She's in bed with gout'. 'What!' said the other ancient aviator, 'not old Tommy Gout of twenty-three squadron?'

There was a boom in air-taxi work straight after the war and at one time at least forty of these mini-airlines were based at Gatwick Airport. Some remarkable enterprises were started and looking back on those days of unsuitable short-range aircraft with hardly any radio, I have come to the conclusion that we were all utterly mad. One mate of mine, who had been a radio operator in Bomber Command during the war, joined a small outfit making regular flights

to South Africa in small twin-engined aircraft that were totally inadequate for the purpose. There was a pilot up front and my friend sat next to him, acting as radio operator. Behind the two crew sat six trusting customers. The little bird only had a safe range of about 500 miles, so, many landings were made on the way down to Johannesburg.

One refuelling stop was at a primitive airstrip in darkest Africa. It was so hot, the local lads, who humped the drums of petrol and pumped it into the tanks by hand, walked around in their birthday suits, wearing not even a pocket handkerchief. They were also particularly well developed, in every meaning of the expression. On the trip I have in mind, the plane landed in the usual cloud of dust, taxied in and the engines were shut down. My mate, the radio operator, walked to the back of the little cabin, opened the door, put out the ladder and descended, ready to offer a helping hand. Two of these exceptionally well-endowed refuelling staff were walking towards the plane just as one of the passengers appeared in the doorway of the cabin. This worthy, a retired colonel from Texas, took one look at them and said, 'Well goddam! If mah wife sees this she'll think ah'm dee-formed.'

Of course, military pilots were not the only ones to apply their wartime skills in a civil capacity. There was this highly skilled RAF fitter who became a warrant officer in charge of the maintenance at a big bomber station. With the return of peace, he got himself a job in a big aircraft factory. It was one of those places where technology was changing so rapidly that they had notices everywhere which said *If it works, it's obsolete.* However, one day, after he had been there only a few weeks, the ex-WO burst into the works manager's office in some distress and said, 'That's it; give me my cards, I'm off. I've had enough. Those men of yours on the shop floor are all queers.'

'What on earth are you talking about?' asked the works manager, 'How can you make such claims when you have only been here two weeks? Look, I can see that you are overwrought; perhaps it is the sudden change from service life to civvie street? Mavis (and he turned to his secretary) give the man a cigarette and a cup of tea.'

They chatted quietly for about ten minutes and then the works manager said to the ex-WO, 'Well now, are you feeling any happier about your job here?' to which the man replied, 'Yes, I suppose I am.' 'Well then,' answered the works manager, 'give us a kiss and go back to work.'

The Army is mainly interested in liaison with the troops in the field and there has been a long line of light, spotter planes that have been built for the purpose. Like most things aeronautical, over the years these spotter planes have tended to become larger and heavier. I remember looking at a big, tough-looking Army aircraft, built like a tank and all in khaki. The major who was showing it to me said, 'Nice bird – strong as a house. What it can't climb over, it demolishes.'

These days the Army operates a fleet of helicopters and on one occasion it held a large exercise. Seamen and airmen report their position either as a latitude and a longitude or they may use a bearing and distance from a known point. Not so the Army. Their pride and joy is the Army Grid, a pattern of numbered and lettered squares overprinted on maps. The 'brown jobs' report their positions in the form of a map reference consisting of letters and numbers. On this occasion, the chopper boys were each given a map reference and told to land there. Nearby would be a public telephone box. Included in their instructions was a telephone number which the pilot was to ring in order to obtain further instructions for the next stage of the exercise.

One of the Army pilots was detailed to take his commanding officer, a very stiff-upper-lip colonel, with him as an observer. They wind up the chopper, lift off and the young pilot map reads his way to the Army Grid reference he has been given. He and his colonel are rather surprised to find that it coincides with the parade-ground at a large RAF station, where a ceremony is taking place with line upon line of RAF personnel standing smartly to attention. However, the instructions said 'land' and there was the public telephone standing by the side of the NAAFI building.

There is considerable downwash from the rotor of a chopper which spreads outwards as it nears the ground, hardly surprising really because it has nowhere else to go. As the chopper prepared to land, RAF hats were blowing everywhere, including that of the rather senior-looking officer who was taking the parade. The young Army pilot switched off the engine and ran to the telephone box with the number he had been given.

A few minutes later he returned with a red face and said, 'Sorry, sir – bit of a mix-up – just been trying to 'phone the map reference – afraid we have landed on the telephone number.'

After the war, a number of Americans came back to visit the places they had known during the war. There were many US bomber stations in East Anglia and one evening an ex-Flying Fortress pilot walked into a beautiful fifteenth-century pub (of the low, oak-beamed ceiling variety) and bought himself a double Scotch. During the war the pub had been full of Yankee airmen, many of them in flying jackets decorated with pictures the likes of which you would not show to your maiden aunt. The majority of them sported a mammoth cigar, fixed permanently in the corner of the mouth. Some of them even took lunch and dinner thus adorned. It was all part of the kit. Now the war was over and the place was deserted, except for two typically English country gentlemen, sitting in their tweeds at the far end of the room. In the corner was a pair of 12-bore guns and two Labradors lay asleep by a big log fire.

Our American mate advanced on this scene of rural tranquillity and said, 'Good evening, gentleman. I've just come over from the States and I'm on my own. D'you mind if I siddown?' To which one of the country gents placed a monocle in his right eye and replied, 'Not at all, old boy, do. Please make yourself at home. But you must excuse my brother; he's a little bit deaf.' Now that was the understatement of the year because his brother was as deaf as a post and as country gent number one shrieked 'Henry, the gentleman has just come over from the United States' (in a voice that could be heard in the next county), dear Henry sat there, mouth open and hand to ear, nodding his head to confirm 'receiving you loud and sometimes clear'. From then on the conversation went something like this:

Country gent to Yankee airman: 'Have you been over here before?'

YA to CG: 'Yeah – yeah. I was here durin' the war.'

CG to Henry: 'HENRY – the gentleman was here during the war.' At which point he turns to the American and says, 'I suppose you were with the US Navy.'

YA to CG: 'Hell no, sir, US Army Air Force.'

CG to Henry: 'HENRY – the gentleman came over with the US Air Force.' To which brother Henry nodded with his mouth even wider open than before.

At this point in the conversation, the country gent felt moved to ask if his new American friend had been stationed anywhere near the pub; to which he replied that his squadron had been based on the big airfield now lying empty just a few miles down the road. While he was stationed here, had he met any local families, the Englishman politely enquired. Yes, indeed he had; and they were all very kind and hospitable, came the reply, and that provoked another question.

CG to YA: 'Well, talking of local people, old boy, did you ever meet Lady Plumbley?'

YA to CG: 'Why, goddamit – I used to sleep with Lady Plumbley night after night!'

CG to Henry: 'Oh HENRY – the gentleman knows mother, *very well.*'

Down under, the end of the war released into Australian society an infusion of high-spirited ex-aircrew with not enough to do with their time. Rather than make an honest living, some of these worthies went barnstorming. They got together a collection of war-surplus aircraft, many in a tatty condition, and put on airshows wherever a local airfield was foolish enough to have them. The tents, flags and bunting would go up, the loudspeakers and barriers appeared and, following a little publicity in the right quarters, the locals flocked in to watch the show.

The highlight came when a Strine voice announced, 'Lydies an' gennelmen, your lawcal mayor has agreed to make a parachute jump for charity. Give 'im a big 'and.' The fact that His Worship the Mayor was known to have a pathological dislike of aircraft, hated crowds and became dizzy standing on a carpet with thick pile was neither here nor there. For, over on the right was an old biplane taking off, the pilot waving from his open cockpit. It would climb up and return over the centre of the airfield at about 2,000 feet. Then the pilot would throw out a large sack with a rope tied around the middle, so that it vaguely resembled a human figure. This fell to the ground and landed with a sickening thud in front of the crowd, while women fainted and children screamed. Some people have a distorted idea of humour.

In a totally different class is the very impressive air display which takes place at Farnborough every two years. A professional commentator explains every move as the latest 'wonderplanes', civil and military, do their stuff. At a time when the Hawker Hunter was one of the most potent jet fighters in the world, it was being displayed by that outstanding company test pilot, Bill Bedford. The pride of the RAF appeared, low down, flying at about 700 mph with visible shock waves coming off the wings and the commentator, his voice shaking with emotion, said, 'And here comes Bill Hunter in his Bedford.'

Current ace commentator at Farnborough and other air shows is a character of aviation, by name of John Blake, who has a massive dark moustache which cracks like a whip on a windy day. He is a big man in the James Robertson Justice mould, with a voice to match. Some time ago, he was on the judging panel at the World Aerobatic Championship competition which, that year, was being held in Russia. At one stage of the event, he felt the Russians were bending the rules to their own advantage. So he demanded that the competition be stopped until all nations could be persuaded to use the same rule book. And stop it they did. When I later discussed the incident with a mutual friend, he said, 'I am not surprised John had the Russians standing to attention. They probably thought it was the return of Peter the Great.'

Unfortunately, John lost his right hand in a bomb-disposal accident, so whenever he wishes to make the usual vulgar two-finger sign, all that comes up is a stump which is usually accompanied by words such as 'that will teach me to change the fan belt with the engine running.'

Several Farnboroughs ago, John was giving his usual informative and perfectly timed commentary. One of those remarkable short take-off and landing (STOL) aircraft was doing its stuff and John was saying, 'Now ladies and gentlemen, I want you to pay particular attention to this show-stopper because the pilot can always be relied upon to produce a spectacular landing.' A split second after he had uttered the word 'landing', the pilot flew straight into the runway, the wings dropped off, two balls of fire engulfed the engines (but fortunately went out immediately) and the unhurt crew abandoned ship with commendable alacrity. I was talking to John shortly afterwards and he was full of praise for his assistant in the commentary box. 'Do you know, when the crash occurred, he managed to switch off my microphone just before I said "Oh s**t!" '

A few hours later, a large crane appeared to remove the wreckage. The chap on the ground, whose job it was to attach the crane's hook to the remains of the aircraft, looked up at the man in his control cab and said, 'Oi! – do you want a wing or a leg?'

Often, when I have given talks in various parts of the world, I am approached afterwards by members of the audience who are anxious to acquaint me of their aviation connections. After one occasion in the north of England, a rather spotty lad with a thick Liverpool accent came up to me and said: 'Ay. Me father wuz in de Aar Ay Eff, 'e flew over Germany and dropped ten tuns of bombs and when 'e gorrome dey put 'im in gaol.'

'Why did they put him in gaol for dropping bombs on Germany?' I asked.

'Well 'e did it last week.'

I close this account of the immediate post-war years with another story about giving talks to appreciative audiences. The fact is that, straight after the war, it was very fashionable for people who had taken an active part in the Battle of the Atlantic, the Bomber Offensive, or some major land campaign, to be invited as guest speakers by Rotary Clubs, Women's Institutes and schools. There was this frightfully up-market girls' school in an exclusive area of London. The headmistress had been told of a very gallant Polish fighter pilot who had flown during the Battle of Britain. For political reasons he was unable to return home and he was now living not far from the school.

The headmistress wrote him a letter which went as follows:

Dear Flight Lieutenant Wisnanski

I understand you took an active part in the Battle of Britain, flying alongside our brave boys in blue [yuck]. The girls at this school would love you to come and talk of your experiences.

Yours sincerely,

Irma Lush
Headmistress, St Prudence Academy for Girls

It so happens that Wisnanski (in Poland the name is spelt Wiclnaxywclanski, but for the purpose of this story and in the interest of paper economy, I will use the British equivalent) was very shy, particularly modest about his achievements and his English was not all that good anyway. So he wrote back:

Dear Madam,

Please excuse. No speak very well the English handwriting. Thank you.

Good bye,

Wiclnaxywclanski

Now being a very determined headmistress, Miss Lush went round to see the gallant Pole. 'Flight Lieutenant, I know it is very naughty of me,' she said, 'but I have promised the girls you will come and talk to them. P-l-e-a-s-e don't disappoint us all.' Well, being a gallant Pole he reluctantly agreed, but the prospect of standing up and talking in public, even to a room full of little girls, filled him with apprehension. So before setting out for the school, he tanked himself up from a suitable bottle.

Now picture the situation. The assembly hall of this frightfully expensive private school is packed with nice girls from up-market families. There they are in eager anticipation, dressed in their beautiful white and pale blue uniforms, the little ones in a semicircle on the floor, the older ones on chairs behind and the senior girls on a raised platform at the back. Before them stands Wisnanski, gyrating unsteadily and breathing pungent gin fumes over the little girls. He has come to the climax of his Battle of Britain epic and the punch lines are about to go in. Now when a Pole speaks broken English with a thick accent, it is not easy to understand and even more difficult to convey on paper. But to the best of my ability, this is what he said:

'Ven all of a suddenly forty Fokkers came from ze left! Forty Fokkers came from ze right! And another forty Fokkers came from ze frontings!'

It was at this point that many of the older girls at the back started giggling and the headmistress felt moved to interrupt the talk so that she could do some explaining.

'Girls,' said the knowledgeable Miss Lush, 'perhaps I should explain, if our speaker will not object, that during the war the Focke-Wulf 190 was a very successful German fighter.'

'Jess,' exploded Wisnanski, stabbing a corrective finger towards the headmistress, 'but deze Fokkers was Messershmitts.'

VEN SUDDENLY FORTY FOKKERS CAME FROM ZE LEFT!

Chapter 3

THE AIRLINE TYPES

Trades develop different types of people. There can be no doubt about this whatsoever. As experts in the art of non-committal description, motor dealers are approached only by estate agents. Lawyers and members of the medical profession are so clever (they would have us more simple mortals believe), they often baffle one another; while you can always recognise a plumber on holiday: he is the one who has to go back for his luggage.

In the main, the aviation mob are thoroughly nice people although, in my experience, some are definitely nicer than others. There are the airline directors, many of whom eventually suffer ulcers, and the directors of firms making aircraft, who get ulcers on their ulcers. Of course, aviation is all about aeroplanes; without them there would be no need for all those ulcers on the ground and we would still be spending weeks aboard ships, although a letter from London to New York would arrive just as quickly, if you will pardon my misuse of the word. Before World War 2, when all Transatlantic mail went by sea, it took the same five days as it does in our age of high tech.

Now, the aeroplane really does represent another world and the folk who crew them are, in my view, a particularly nice breed. Top of the tree is, of course, the captain – his arms laden with four gold rings, his pilots' log-book bulging with many thousands of flying hours and his brief-case containing enough maps to paper the parlour. Modern pilots are, in the main, pretty smooth characters and quite different from the old pioneers who sat in open cockpits while their passengers were being violently sick in their wicker chairs. These weather-beaten mariners of the air used to develop skins of leather. I remember one famous old airline skipper who became so wrinkled they had to screw his flying helmet on and off.

Today's airline captain will have come up through the ranks – flying school, perhaps a spell as a flying instructor, second officer (i.e. a junior captain's assistant under training), first officer and eventually that much sought-after captaincy in the left-hand seat. But take my tip, dear readers, never fly with *any* pilot unless he has got grey hair. In general, the senior crew of a large airliner will be made up as follows:

- *Captain*. Knows he is God and expects to be recognised as such. Thinks all first officers are upstarts to be kept under the strictest supervision. Only speaks to the flight engineer via the first officer or, very occasionally, the purser. Looking forward to his imminent retirement and that inflation-proof, fire-proof, index-linked pension. With it he will enjoy alcoholic days with other retired airline captains at the local golf-club.
- *First officer*. Thinks the captain is God but has a feeling he is really past it and needs the assistance of a young chap of character who is endowed with the utmost professional skill (himself). Inclined to mistrust flight engineers and looks forward to the day when he is a captain, so that he can snub the breed.
- *Flight engineer*. Is prepared to acknowledge that, if there is a God it is probably the captain, but quite certain the old chap is past it. Sits sideways, facing an enormous instrument/control panel many times larger than the one entrusted to the pilots. Is responsible for management of the fuel, electrics, pressurisation, etc. and also helps by tuning the radio for the pilots. Thinks no pilot can tell a propeller from a tailplane (some modern jet pilots have actually *never* flown

behind a prop) and is not looking forward to anything in particular, except the nicely built blonde serving gin and tonics in the first-class lounge. Is dreading the day when the first officer becomes a captain.

- *Purser/Manager*. These days, aircraft have become large enough to follow ship's practice. The purser (sometimes known as the manager) is responsible to the captain for the smooth running of the gin-and-tonic areas. In a big plane, there will be three of these: First Class, Business Club Class and Tourist/Economy. He has a staff of male and female stewards, although some will be in the Middlesex Regiment. Before aircraft became big enough to have a purser/manager, a senior girl ran the cabin staff and one airline included the following words in its staff instructions' book: 'The position of the Senior Stewardess is immediately under the Captain.'

Of course, all this is not to be taken too seriously. In fact, the flight-deck and cabin crew must work closely as a team, for safety's sake if for no other reason; but pilots, in particular, have had to face the challenge of fast-growing technology the like of which has no equal in any other walk of life. Furthermore, these days there are no radio operators or navigators, so the pilots have to share these tasks along with the basic one of flying the hardware. Before flight engineers were introduced to relieve the pilots of some tasks, so many dials were appearing on their instrument panels that one magazine printed a cartoon which showed a captain and his first officer in their seats on the flight-deck. Before them is an array of dials that would do justice to a major power-station and the skipper is saying to his first officer, 'Haven't a clue what they are all for, old boy, but that one in the top right-hand corner gives damn good Stock Exchange reports.'

In the days before jets, when it was by no means unknown for the massive piston engines of the period to go on strike, often announcing the fact in a somewhat vocal manner, one dear old captain, who had become a legend within and outside the profession, was a guest on a television chat show. What future developments, asked the interviewer, would you like to see in aviation. 'My dear young chap,' the senior skipper answered, 'I look forward to the day when my flight engineer says "Captain, number eight engine has just packed up", and I reply "Which number eight, port or starboard?" '

That same senior captain had a rather odd habit which was a topic of debate among the first officers who flew with him. At the start of a flight, the old chap would taxi on to the runway and line up on the centre line, which is marked with a series of painted dashes like a road. Then he would pick up a brief-case, open it, look inside, close it again and replace it on the floor. The ritual never changed and it would be followed by an immaculate take-off and a faultless instrument departure (i.e. the prescribed route to be flown from the airport when joining the airways system). It was all copy-book stuff.

Then came the time when this highly respected captain retired and his colleagues threw a big party for him. They got him slightly drunk and, while he was thus disadvantaged, a few of the young first officers got his brief-case and opened it. Inside the flap, in copperplate letters, were written those immortal words: *Port is Left and Starboard is Right*.

While on the subject of senior skippers, a near neighbour of mine, who used to be the captain of a large cruise liner, tells the story of a night when among his privileged guests at the 'Captain's Table' was a German gentleman. Although he was wearing glasses with lenses like the bottom of a beer bottle, the gentleman was nevertheless

reading the menu with it held about an inch from his nose. The conversation went something like this:

Ship's Captain: 'What do you do for a living, may I ask?'

Passenger: '*Ja* – I am a senior training captain with our famous international airline, Hansafahdt.'

Ship's Captain: 'A senior airline captain!'

Passenger: '*Ja* – I know vat you are sinking. Mein eyes are not very goot. But zer ears are perfect. Unt now everyzink on zer aeroplane is outomatick. If I fly to zer left of track, it goes 'PING'. If I go to zer right, it goes 'DONG'. If zer aeroplane is too high, it makes zer sound 'TING–A–LING–A–LING' unt if I fly too low, a recorded voice says 'WOOP–WOOP, PULL UP'. So ve go flying along zer routes wiz everything going 'PING',

'DONG', 'TING-A-LING-A-LING', 'WOOP-WOOP, PULL UP'.

By now the Ship's Captain and his other guests were on the edge of their seats, wondering what to expect next. The German continued:

'At zer destination, mein virstofficer says "Herr Kapitan, zer airfield is directly below zer aircraft". So I klose zer throttles unt dive, unt dive, unt dive until near zer ground mein virstofficer covers his face wiz his hants and screams D-Aaaaaah! Zen I move zer wheel back unt land zer aeroplane.'

Flight-deck crews, particularly the pilots, are well paid. And so they should be. Their responsibilities are great; their training costs more than that of a doctor; their working life is relatively short and there is always the risk of being grounded because some doctor finds an unexplained squiggle on the poor chap's cardiograph trace. Professional pilots have medicals at six-monthly intervals and there was this Polish airline captain whose aircraft was stuck at London Airport for want of a spare part which had to come from Warsaw. The delay was a nuisance, because it so happened that his medical certificate was due to run out before he could fly the repaired aircraft back to Warsaw.

Fortunately the airline world operates on a 'you-help-me and I'll-help-you' basis, so the Polish airline captain duly presented himself at the medical department of a well-known British airline. Naturally the medical exam includes an eyesight test, so the doctor stood the Polish skipper before the test card, got him to cover one eye and said, 'Can you read the bottom line?'

'Read it!' replied the Pole in a mixture of surprise and delight, 'I know him.'

Captains of large aircraft operated by the major airlines live pretty comfortably, but sometimes their wives get carried away and think they are married to millionaires. There was this very attractive captain's other half who was a compulsive spender. Her husband was having a few days off when a large bill arrived in the morning post for still more expensive dresses. The skipper blew a fuse, played Hamlet with his wife, stormed out of the house and disappeared in the direction of the local golf-club.

Half-way round the course, he began to feel badly about bawling out his wife, so he curtailed the game, jumped into his car and drove home. There was no sign of his wife on the ground floor so he went upstairs and there she was, lying on the bed in her birthday suit without a stitch of clothing on.

'What on earth are you doing?' enquired the airline skipper in utter astonishment.

'Well, I have taken to heart everything you have said about my overspending. So to make my clothes last longer, I have decided to spend several hours every day lying naked on the bed,' replied our heroine.

'I have never heard such utter rubbish in my life,' said the airline captain. He walked across the room to where an entire wall was covered with built-in wardrobes. There he slid back two of the eight doors to reveal line upon line of expensive gowns. 'Having to save your clothes – look at all these. There is your grey chiffon, your blue Dior, your favourite Jaeger outfits, your – hallo Charlie – your brown two-piece.'

Not all first officers graduate to the exalted rank of captain and some, in my experience, do not deserve to. I have in mind one unfortunate chap who was so ignorant that he thought an innuendo was an Italian suppository. He had a persecution complex that did not improve when he visited his GP and complained, 'Doctor, there must be something wrong with me because none of my colleagues will speak to me', whereupon the doctor called, 'Next patient please'.

DOCTOR, THERE MUST BE SOMETHING WRONG WITH ME BECAUSE NONE OF MY COLLEAGUES WILL SPEAK TO ME.
NEXT PATIENT PLEASE.

Not long after joining an airline, they sent him on a trip with a captain who was so tough he used to chew nails and spit rust. That captain was known to eat first officers for breakfast.

It was a night flight, the weather was foul and they were coming in to land at London Gatwick. Perhaps I should explain that under such circumstances, with cloud and rain obscuring the ground, the pilot is guided towards the runway on a descending path by a radio approach aid called Instrument Landing System (ILS). It is very accurate but unless it is a large jet with Autoland (fully automatic landing), the final part of the deal entails breaking through cloud, making visual contact with the approach lighting, which is there to guide one to the beginning of the runway, then landing with reference to the surface and the aircraft's landing lights.

The usual cockpit procedure is for the pilot flying the approach to concentrate on the instruments while the other one peers out of the windows, ready to shout 'LIGHTS' as soon as the welcome sight appears. On the occasion I am describing, they approached Gatwick with the rain doing an impersonation of Noah's Flood and everything outside blacker than black. 'No bloody messing, boy,' roared the fire-eating captain to his below-standard first officer, 'as soon as you see 'em, I want you to shout "LIGHTS". And don't sod about taking a second look.'

Picture the situation. Captain Fire-eater has his head down, eyes glued to the twitching instruments before him, while First Officer Clot peers through the windscreen. The aircraft gets lower and lower, the rain becomes louder and louder and mounting tension on the flight-deck is finally broken when the first officer shouts 'LIGHTS'. The skipper raises his head and transfers his gaze from the instruments to straight ahead, where all is even blacker than before. 'Where?' he demands. 'They're behind you,' replies our hero. After that he lost his job and joined a small charter firm. He became the only pilot on record to have crashed his plane by backing it into a mountain. I really rather liked the poor chap, but he was from an unfortunate family. His father once lost his glass eye during an all-night marbles tournament.

The policy with most airlines is to have flexible crew rostering. In other words, crews are made up for each flight and because of first-class training, everyone knows his or her job. In so far as flight-deck crews are concerned, senior ones are appointed training captains or training flight engineers. It is the responsibility of these highly skilled aircrew to ensure standardisation throughout the airline. This is vital if crews are to be totally interchangeable. On a big airline, a first officer may rarely fly with the same captain twice a year, but every profession has its characters and there are such folk on the airways who are well known by name and reputation, even to those who have never flown with them.

This little tale is about a flight engineer who was renowned for his pathological dislike of Communists, so much so that he was something of a standing joke among the airline's flight crew personnel, which numbered several thousand pilots and flight engineers. I suppose one day it was bound to happen, but they put him on a flight to Moscow with a crew who knew all about his reputation. During the pre-flight checks at Heathrow, he could be heard quietly fuming about 'Commies', on the long flight he was on about people in black hats who follow you everywhere and by the time they had landed at Moscow, he was seeing KGB agents in every corner.

On the minibus which was taking the crew to its Moscow hotel he had reached the stage of 'You take it from me, mates, they've got microphones everywhere. And I'm telling you straight, if I find any, the b*****s will be smashed.' By now they had arrived at their hotel which, by

Moscow standards, was not a bad pub. A lift that belonged to the propeller rather than the jet age took them to their rooms on the third floor. The flight engineer entered his and immediately started to move the furniture and roll back the carpet. Hallo – hallo – hallo! What's this! There, in the centre of the floor was a black metal plate about eight inches in diameter! In triumph, he rushed from room to room, telling the rest of the crew to 'Cop a load of this and perhaps you will now stop laughing at me because I have found a microphone under the flipping carpet.'

He returned to the bedroom, followed by the rest of the crew, who stood around in a circle, watching in amazement as the flight engineer carefully removed the three screws securing the metal plate. As he removed it everyone from the captain to the most junior stewardess craned forward and there, about six inches below the floor-boards, was a small, black, circular box. 'There's the bastard,' announced our flying Sherlock Holmes. 'I'll teach the KGB to spy on me.'

The box seemed to be held by another three screws and the crew watched in silence as, one by one, he carefully removed the first two. When the last screw was released, there was the most almighty crash as a large glass chandelier crashed down from the ceiling of the bedroom below. Without a word, the flight engineer screwed up all the bits, rolled back the carpet and replaced the furniture.

Talking of hotels reminds me of a mate of mine, by name of Chris Couch, who learned to fly at the same school in Texas as me. (It was an RAF flying school, but they were wise enough to locate it in Terrell, near Dallas and I can assure the reader that we have no complaints on that account.) Like many of my wartime colleagues, Chris became an airline pilot afterwards and by the time he retired he was captain of the biggest type of aircraft then flying.

Chris flew for a large independent airline which specialised in transporting mums, dads and the kids on holiday to once exotic parts of the world. At one time they had a contract flying holiday passengers to and from Malta and those going out used to arrive on the island rather late at night. The crew would stay in an hotel overnight and fly home returning holiday-makers the following morning.

At the end of a flight, there are a number of technical and other reports to be written, refuelling to supervise and oil levels to be checked. So by the time all the formalities had been completed, the crew arrived at their hotel around midnight. Captain Chris liked a Scotch and a smoke before getting his head down and the routine was well known at the hotel; he was, after all, a guest for one night every week during the holiday season. On this occasion he had no matches, so he picked up the telephone in his bedroom and said, 'Please send up a Scotch and a box of matches.'

Five minutes became ten, ten became twenty and there was still no sign of the Scotch and matches. So Chris telephoned again and the concierge said, 'Sorry about the delay Captain Couch, the night porter will be with you in five minutes.' Five minutes became ten, ten became twenty and still no Scotch and matches. Another telephone call produced the same profuse apologies and promises of instant service which never materialised.

By now it was almost one in the morning – long past the skipper's bedtime. He ripped the telephone wire off the wall, went down in the lift and stood before the concierge in his striped pyjamas, telephone in hand with two yards of wire trailing along the floor. Chris Couch looks more like the chairman of a public company than an airline pilot and by now he was red in the face with anger. 'Captain Couch,' stuttered the concierge in terror, 'whatever is the matter?'

'I want another telephone,' growled the captain, 'this one lies.'

CAPTAIN COUCH, WHAT EVER IS THE MATTER?
I WANT ANOTHER TELEPHONE, THISONE LIES!!!
G
1
2
3
4
CC

By and large the flight-deck and cabin crews employed by the major airlines are put up in good hotels when working on the longer routes that demand an overnight stop. But all pilots are not airline captains. Some earn their crust flying a private company jet or turboprop; while others are employed by modest air-taxi firms that often operate small twin-engined aircraft capable of carrying six to eight passengers. Such worthies may well be seen wearing smart uniforms with gold rings on their sleeves, but the economics of air-taxi flights rarely permit the use of good class hotels when the crew have to make an overnight stop.

I am reminded of an air-taxi friend of mine who once flew some people to Blackpool, where he had to make an overnight stop. The better hotels were full and so were the private ones; consequently he was forced to stay in a boarding-house used primarily by commercial travellers. On the wall of the bedroom was a notice, written in the fair hand of the landlady, which said: 'Guests using the chamber-pots are requested not to park them under the bed since the steam rusts the springs'. Which sounds like a reasonable enough request to me.

Chapter 4

COPING WITH AIRPORTS

A friend of mine used to say that you are not safe anywhere outside a pub. Now, while many would consider that to be a sweeping overstatement, few would deny that the comfortable certainties of pre-war days have mostly disappeared. Nowadays, British postage stamps are so expensive you sometimes have to pay by cheque and delivery is such that it is often quicker to wait until you next meet the recipient. Our railways were a model of efficiency; the trains were cheap; they were among the fastest in the world and you could set your watch when the 12.55 pulled out of your local station. Now, although British Rail insist on telling us 'WE ARE (still) GETTING THERE', there is no point in looking at your watch because odds are the train has been cancelled.

Among the great British declines is the standard of its architects. They always had a tendency to put aesthetics before practicalities, but now even that has gone for a loop; today we have architects who consider it the 'in' thing to display all the plumbing outside the building. The Stock Exchange is a prime example (I've heard of outside sanitation but this is ridiculous). And when are they going to finish the NatWest skyscraper in the City of London? You know the one I mean – the builders have left a massive black box on the roof.

The day they let architects anywhere near aviation was an utter disaster. You have only to visit the airports of the world to realise that architects who have flipped their lids are an international problem, because most airports have these features in common.

Car-parks

These are usually available in two flavours, known as 'short term' and 'long term'. The former is within a marathon walk of the passenger terminal and may cost you an arm and a leg; whereas the second alternative, which is slightly less expensive, may be located in the next county. The long-term car-parks are very badly signposted and you are led, via numerous roundabouts, past five or six vast enclosures, most of them empty but all declared *Full*, until time running out and in some panic, you find a slot. An airport courtesy bus collects you and delivers passengers to the various terminal buildings (yours will certainly be last), but with a following wind you should arrive at the check-in desk ten minutes before flight departure. Parking the car is likely to be the most exciting part of the trip.

The passenger terminal

This is another world. Usually the fare-paying customers enter through doors that open automatically and threaten to grab you by the brief-case (or worse) if you dare linger. Along the walls are the check-in desks, batches of them for each airline with separate positions for the various destinations. At a big, international airport, all the famous names are there – Air Fungus, Quaintarse, BO Airways, Air Trance, Dan Dare, the giant Russian airline, Aeroclot and Swizzair, a well-run airline from a well-run country (in Switzerland, efficiency means everything and they even put bells on the cows because their horns don't work). At the airport there are bright electric signs everywhere and among the posters will very likely be one advertising a famous airline which proclaims 'Breakfast in London – Lunch in New York', to which should be added 'Luggage in Tokyo'.

The passenger terminal will have various snack-bars and an establishment that calls itself a restaurant (sic). At one airport known to me, the food was so bad the flies in the

CAR
PARK

kitchen used to commit suicide (just like their ancestors at RAF Padgate during the war) and pygmies made a habit of coming all the way from Africa just to dip their arrows in the soup. This is particularly sad because the chef at this airport is a workaholic – if you mention work, he gets himself drunk. One of the waitresses once told me 'You can tell he is a hardened drinker; he's got mouldy boots and a rusty zip'. Everywhere you look, people in uniforms are rushing around with those portable, cordless telephones, talking to officials in remote offices and receiving cryptic messages. A mate of mine used to have one of these cordless wonders at home, but he had to get rid of his because the dog kept burying it.

Public Announcement System

At frequent intervals loudspeakers in the passenger lounge will go 'BING–BOING' and a charming female voice, every next word delivered in high alternated with low pitch to confuse the foreigners, will warn the customers that the time has come to gather up the duty free and aim towards their wonderplane. You should be able to understand about one word in ten and a typical example might be: 'BING–BOING! Macclesfield International Airways flight number VAT sixty-nine to Worksop now boarding from gate twenty-four' (which is almost certainly on the other side of the airport).

Of course, we may be British but we do cater for foreigners at our airports and the various airlines often put out announcements in their native tongues. I am not much good at languages myself, but from time to time you are likely to hear something that sounds rather like this: 'BING–BOING! Senior a senoria, Cascara Aerovias huida de Flushing marcharse hacia puerta cuatro poko moko, preygo, preygo'; or for the benefit of German passengers: 'BING–BOING! Achtung! Hansafahdt flug funfuntzwantsig zu Dumbkopfberg unt Baden-Baden ist von thor zehn geben; raus-raus, schnell – schnell!' In either case, British (certainly English) travellers are advised to ignore these announcements.

Behind the scenes

All manner of things are going on behind closed doors at a big modern airport. Most important, perhaps, is the air-traffic control department which is situated in a tall, thin building with a commanding view of the runways. Like most things aviation, words mean what they say and the tall thin office is called a tower.

There are a number of controllers in the tower, each speaking on a different radio frequency and each addressed by a different name. For example, the chap who controls aircraft taxiing is appropriately called 'Ground'; the one handling air traffic departing and landing is called 'Tower' and as you arrive from afar or depart from the airport, the chap to speak to is addressed as 'Approach'. I was once in the tower at Biggin Hill when an attractive female voice asking for landing instructions caused something of a hiatus when she asked the controller, 'Would you like me on the grass or on the runway?'

Chapter 7 is devoted to radio chat, so I will confine myself here to saying that there was a time when the air-traffic control (ATC) service in Britain was so officious that it became known among pilots as the RSPCA (the Royal Society for the Prevention of Civil Aviation). Fortunately for us all, attitudes have changed and in my experience the boys and girls in ATC are almost as splendid as the flight-deck and cabin crews.

Not all air terminals are big airports like Paris Charles de Gaulle, London Heathrow or New York J.F. Kennedy. Some are simple to the point of being primitive. For example, what was once called British European Airways used to operate the Scottish island services. One port of call was Barra (the island of *Whisky Galore* fame) where, to this day, the 'airport' consists of three landing strips marked in the sand. At high tide these disappear and, in the days I have in mind, it was the responsibility of the local station manager, a lady of sound judgement, to telephone the mainland when Barra Airport was fit to receive aircraft. This she decided by watching the seagulls on the beach. If she could see their legs, the water was shallow enough and it was all systems go.

In those days there were a few characters among the pilots and one captain, who was banished to the remote inter-island services because he was an incurable practical joker, used to liven up the passengers before take-off by walking through the cabin, tapping his way to the flight-deck with a white stick. His other favourite party piece was to sit among the passengers in a raincoat which hid his uniform. About five minutes after departure time, he would look at his watch and say, 'this is not good enough, keeping us waiting like this.' Then he would walk into the flight-deck of the little passenger plane used on the Scottish island routes, leave the door open, look quickly through a technical book and then tell the petrified passengers, 'Well, I think I've got the hang of it. We have all been kept waiting long enough and since the pilot has not turned up, I'll have a go myself.' With that, he would start up and take off, while the passengers gripped their seats in terror.

Another important 'back room' operation is the Met Office. For many years meteorology was, for good reason, described as an 'inexact science', because nothing is more non-committal than a Met man giving a weather forecast. You know the sort of thing we used to hear on the radio: 'It will be cool in Poole and dry in Rye, but if you are visiting Lissingdown you are advised to take an umbrella'.

And remember the early days of television, before they

TAP
TAP

had those wonderful instant, ever-changing charts? There were rather crude maps painted on metal boards with magnetic letters and numbers which they moved about to show the temperature, wind and weather. On one occasion the letter 'F' had fallen off the beginning of a word and it said 'og'. The television producer managed to draw this to the attention of the chap giving the weather report. He turned around, recognised the problem and then promptly said, 'Sorry about the F–in–fog'.

These days, a modern Met office is all fax machines and computers with reports coming in from all over the world. However, I often feel the forecasters would be more reliable if they changed their seaweed more often.

Boarding the aircraft

At the check-in counters, service is very similar to that at any post office: long queues take an age to move as the staff read every comma on your tickets, punch in code words on the computer, receive more code words back, weigh the baggage, attach labels and offer you seats in the smoking or non-smoking areas. Hence the old saying, 'time to spare – go by air'.

These are wicked days and you will not be allowed very far from the check-in desks before they subject you to a security check. Your hand baggage must go through an X-ray machine while you walk through an electronic door frame which protests in its electronic voice if you are carrying so much as a few bob of loose change. Modern X-ray machines do not damage your camera film, unlike the early ones that did. A mate of mine once took hundreds of shots in the Kruger National Park in South Africa, but instead of the expected wildlife pictures all he got was an inside view of his electric razor.

The next part of the deal is where the architects play a leading role. Because almost without exception passengers who have checked in will be directed upstairs to the departure lounge. This is rarely, if ever, on the ground floor; so simple an arrangement would spoil the little game that has been devised by architects for the entertainment of us all. It entails the following rules:

1. The down escalator must always be running while the one going up is permanently out of order.
2. All passengers must go up a floor so that they can later descend to ground level. But for this, it would be impossible to ensure that they must eventually climb up fifty or so steps leading into the aircraft when the more convenient mobile covered gangways (called jetways) are not available.
3. By a process of clever planning, brilliant to the point of genius, all baggage trolleys required while departing will be at the aircraft end of the terminal building. Passengers arriving at the airport will also find that the trolleys are in the Departure Lounge instead of at the baggage reclaim.
4. All departure gates, whatever their number, must lead the passengers along a series of corridors that entail walking to the very end of the aircraft line. I have it on good authority that aircraft nearer the airport never move; they are set permanently in concrete. Some of the larger airports have moving pavements which run at a speed cunningly selected to deceive the more impatient who, not content with the fact they they are being transported at a fast trot, insist on walking along the moving belt. Sooner or later one must return to solid ground and at the end of the moving pavement the combined velocities have been known to produce a heap of humanity that looks like an outsized rugger scrum.

Airport baggage trolleys are unique and certainly not to be confused with your domesticated supermarket variety.

These airport trolleys have been trained to hide from the passengers and, when found, steer in a pre-programmed direction irrespective of the 'driver'. I have only recently learned that these trolleys are produced by the same firm that manufactures those toilet rolls which refuse to tear along the perforations.

The return home

The terminal building is split into departure (from whence you left) and arrival sections. On your return home, you get off the plane, do the Lands End to John O'Groat's trek in reverse direction and show your passport at emigration control before another fifteen-minute walk to the baggage reclaim, a large hall with a number of conveyor belts wafting gently around and not a trolley in sight.

Baggage tumbles on to the belt and goes walkabout, to use an Australian expression. Some very odd things appear on those baggage conveyors, many of them examples of a touching faith in the gentle hand of the baggage staff, who spend their working day on the other side of the wall, humping baggage off trucks and on to the conveyor belts. Thus, you will often see burst-open parcels spewing out oranges or dirty washing, not to mention cases (tied up with string) with ties or trouser legs dangling out. I even once saw a large cage with a green parrot inside which kept shouting 'If this is the twist; give me a foxtrot every time!'. For some reason, this garbage of the baggage reclaim never seems to be owned by anyone and it goes round and round and round until an official slings it on to the floor in disgust.

Assuming they let you through customs with that Spanish bottle opener you bought for Uncle Jo and the castanets for the kids (those things can ruin your nails, by the way), the next hurdle is to find your car. This is a problem because all airport car-parks look the same and in the panic of leaving you most likely forgot to make a note of

the pick-up point and parking row. You may even find that your cream Cortina is not the only one there and the holiday could end with a conducted tour of the long-term parking area while you try to remember your car's registration.

Flying clubs

At all but the largest and busiest airports there will be one or more flying club(s). Contrary to popular belief, these establishments are not patronised exclusively by millionaires. Indeed, many of the members are relatively young, permanently hard up and prepared to go without holidays and even food so that they can learn to fly and perhaps one day become airline pilots.

Apart from teaching people to fly, some clubs offer joy-rides and on a nice day you will often see people queuing for a quick look at the local area from the air. At one of the seaside resorts, a chap who sold joy-ride tickets used to shout, 'There are only two thrills in life, madam. One of them is flying and for the other one see our pilot after eight tonight'.

In my time I have done quite a lot of joy-riding, and the chap selling the tickets was always warned to be on his best behaviour. In case he was not, I always had a large notice propped up by the entrance to the aircraft. It said: 'We may not always agree, but on this occasion you must not fall out'.

Whatever the social or financial status of an aero-club member, flying can become an obsession which permeates family life. There was this otherwise quite normal chap who joined the local flying club, got himself a Private Pilot's Licence (PPL) and thenceforth spent most of his free time with the aviating fraternity. One Saturday night he came home, nattering on about the latest news at the club when his wife suddenly exploded and said, 'Do you never talk about anything else but flying? It's bad enough that you leave me alone most weekends, but not content with that, you have to come home and go on about your boring flying friends'.

The truth of this outburst struck home and our hero, by nature a reasonable man, said, 'OK – OK, keep your hair on, I'll change the subject if you feel like that. What would you like me to talk about?'

'Anything,' replied the long-suffering memsahib, 'talk about sex if you like, but do us both a favour and keep off flying'.

'All right then, I'll change the subject,' replied the flying fiend, 'I wonder who the chief flying instructor is sleeping with tonight?'

The evils of filthy commerce

I close this discourse on airports with a few words on deregulation, an American invention which, in simple terms, allows a number of airlines to compete on the same routes in a sort of free for all. Like everything in life, deregulation has its good and its bad sides. The good side is the natural human one of competition – nothing like it to keep complacent businesses on their toes. The bad side is that, in an effort to compete on price and service, many of the smaller airlines have cut corners and gone bust or been swallowed up by bigger ones. So if we are not careful, there will be less rather than more competition.

In one big American airport, there are no fewer than ten local airlines with check-in desks and as many as five of them cover the same routes. Not to put too fine a point on it, competition has got out of hand to such a degree that one airline has its ticket girls standing behind the counter topless! One day, a Methodist minister and his wife arrived at the airport. They had planned a few days' holiday in Pittsburgh (rather like you and the wife booking for a weekend break in Sophisticated Scunthorpe) and friends had recommended that very airline which, as an added attraction, employed topless birds in the ticket office. They spotted the name of the airline and when the minister's wife saw the twin-engined talent, she had a touch of the vapours.

'Oh my, Elmer! You can't go over there – just look at

those brazen girls.

'Now now, my dear, don't take on so', replied the man of the cloth. 'They are children of the Almighty just like any other members of my congregation. I shall now go over there and buy our tickets to Pittsburgh – and the girls will not bother me at all.' With those reassuring words, he walked over to the desk, placed himself before a nicely built girl and stuttered, 'Say, er, er, c–can I have two pickets for Tittsburgh?'

So I close this little run-down on airports with a few final words of advice to new air travellers. Allow plenty of time for parking the car, avoid the restaurant, keep your eyes on the arrival and departure boards (they sometimes give the latest cricket scores), listen out for the 'BING–BOING' announcements and, above all else, look out for those topless birds.

Chapter 5

SO YOU ARE OFF TO THE COSTA FORTUNE

Although by 1988 almost eighty-five years had passed since the first successful flight of a heavier-than-air machine (balloons had already been established for some 120 years), a surprisingly large number of people throughout the world have never flown. Among those who have actually committed aviation, a high proportion are the package tour fraternity, many of whom regard the epic of departing from the nearest airport and landing somewhere in the Costa Fortune as something akin to being launched into outer space.

I would be the first to acknowledge and respect the fear of the unknown, but one man's unknown is another's part of everyday life. For example, my GP, who would think nothing of advising folk to have a major by-pass of the fundamental plumbing system (he is very brave when someone else's backside is being carved up), has a pathological fear of flying which, since he is a doctor and I am a professional pilot of many years' experience, I naturally exploit to the maximum.

Please do not misunderstand me; I am not callous about other people's fears. But some of these fears confound all reason. There was, for example, the lady who confronted the check-in clerk at the airport with the words, 'I have never flown before and I am petrified.' The very sympathetic girl said, 'There is nothing at all to worry about, madam. Let me give you a window seat', to which our heroine replied 'No thanks – I can't stand draughts.'

Having survived the nausea of hanging around the airport, the 'BING–BOING' you have been waiting for is

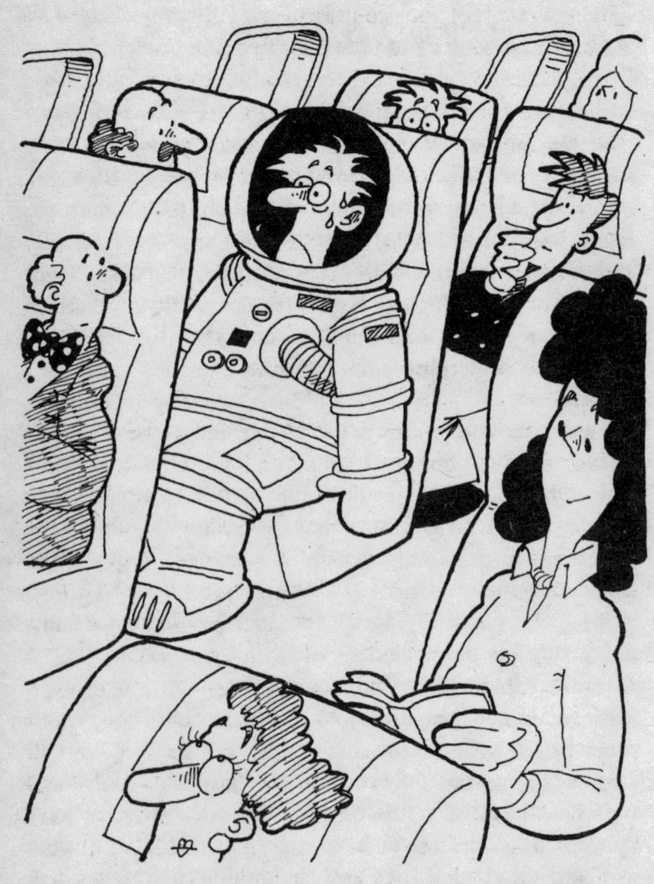

SOME PASSENGERS THINK THEY ARE BEING LAUNCHED INTO OUTER SPACE!

blasted forth on the public-announcement system, followed by a message conveying the general impression that you ought to get out of your seat, gather your bits and pieces and move in the general direction of gate XX.

By now, most of your co-passengers will have collected an assortment of bottles from the duty free shop, weighing in at several thousand pounds and representing enough extra cabin load to add at least another 500 yards to the take-off run.

So, the time comes to depart. The usual passengers who, as a matter of divine right, feel impelled to board the aircraft on the last second of the final minute before they close the doors, have arrived hot and bothered with hair askew. As they are bundled into their seats, the new air travellers are about to experience their first surprise because, instead of moving in the direction of the sharp end, the hardware starts to glide noiselessly backwards.

Push-back is enacted by purpose-built tractors, which also provide temporary electric power for engine starting; so don't be surprised if all the lights flick off and on when they pull the plug and allow the tractor to drive away. (Note: pilots are not allowed to take off with the tractor attached to the aircraft, even for a little joke. It is against union rules.) One airline captain, who was a frustrated Bob Hope, had a habit of coming on the cabin announcement and telling his passengers, 'Ladies and gentlemen, we are now about to reverse. Will you all please sit low in your seats so we can see where we are going.' (Many of the passengers actually did.)

At a busy airport, there may be half-a-dozen or more aircraft taxiing out in procession towards the duty runway. Incidentally, the French have a habit of using the same word for different things and the word *piste* can mean a road, a ski track or a runway. At many French airfields, they often have a notice at the start of the runway in use which says *Piste Service*. For years I used to believe it meant drunk on duty.

In the bad old days before we had jets, heavily laden airliners, their piston engines groaning in protest, would stagger into the air and claw their way slowly upwards while the flight-deck crew silently prayed that the elastic would not break. These days, modern jets have so much surplus power that they climb like a homesick angel with the cabin floor at a steep uphill angle. On one of the first long-distance jet trips I made, a miniature of Scotch I had ordered, and was in process of enjoying, conceded the uphill struggle and fell to the floor. 'Sorry about that, sir,' said one of the stewards as he gave me another bottle, 'the lady up front wants to get there first.'

On the basis that first officers are expected to be future captains, it is usually the practice for 'Sir' in the left-hand seat to allow his number two a proportion of the take-offs and landings. An old captain mate of mine would hog these when the weather was fine but, come thunder and lightning, he would fold his arms, turn to the first officer and say, 'Well, you've got to learn some time my boy.' Usually these up-and-coming future captains are pretty good, although I was on a flight once when the young chap made such a heavy landing that the chief steward burst into tears, rushed on to the flight-deck and hit him with his handbag.

During the flight, public transport aircraft, such as the wonderplane that is taking you to the Costa Fortune, will be confined to a ten-mile wide corridor, called an airway. These railway lines of the air link together the main air centres which cover such places as London, Paris, New York, etc. They are called terminal control areas and others of various shapes and sizes are provided for all busy airports. The charm of all this controlled airspace is that if another aircraft flies into you, while fooling around within an airway without permission, that is against the rules. The pilot will be told off after he hits the ground.

Standards of comfort vary according to the nature of the

flight. If it is a cheap holiday on the Costa Fortune, economics may demand so many rows of seats in the cabin that you are forced to sit with your knees in your navel. Regular, scheduled flights, even in Economy Class, offer adequate if not excessive leg room and Business Class (sometimes called 'Super Club') give you two seats in the width normally occupied by three in the 'Maplins Area'.

There are exceptions but, in the main, airline food is nothing to enthuse about. It comes on board as cold yuck to be placed in electric ovens where it is converted to hot yuck for service to the customers at the appropriate time. The cabin staff then have to push metal trolleys up and down narrow aisles while dishing out the unmentionable to the fare-paying customers. It is no easy task and when some little festerer of a child has been allowed to run wild by its parents, the job can become impossible. I remember when a new stewardess, driven to near murder, asked the 'keepers' of one such festerer if they could get him to play outside.

Not content with selling us air travel by the mile, the airlines of the world insist on flogging perfume and bottles of booze in the air. Often the barrow boy act occurs at the very time one is trying to sleep. One irate passenger, who had been kept awake by an in-flight film she had already seen, had just managed to nod off when the cabin announcement woke her with promises of cheap cigarettes, half bottles of hooch and cachets of Soir de Clapham – all of it duty free. When the trolley arrived with all these goodies, she complained about being kept awake by the constant intrusions. 'It is getting worse all the time, madam,' agreed the sympathetic stewardess. 'From next Monday we'll be selling sweaters too!'

Provided you are not on a short flight, most captains are pleased to accept visitors from the passenger cabin. Usually these take the form of dad and one of the kids standing in awe behind the pilots while the crew point out this and

DO YOU THINK YOU COULD GET YOUR CHILD TO PLAY OUTSIDE

that. One captain, who was well known for his misplaced humour, used to wait until some slightly apprehensive passenger visited the flight-deck. Then he would reach for an AA book, look at the maps and say, 'I wonder if that is Liverpool down there.'

One nervous passenger on a night flight had for more than an hour been watching a red light that could be seen out of the left window so, when he went up to the flight-deck, he pointed to it and said, 'Isn't that red light rather close?' 'I hope so,' replied the captain, 'it's attached to our left wing-tip.' That captain is long since retired, but on his ninetieth birthday they interviewed him on television and asked if, looking back on his interesting life in the air, he had any regrets. The immediate answer was: 'If I had known how long I was going to live, I would have looked after myself better.'

It could be argued that if God had wanted us to fly he would never have given us British Rail but, like it or not, air transport is with us and although the same types of aircraft are often operated by different airlines, the atmosphere from one company to another can be very different. Much too depends on the nationality of the passengers. For example, I once flew from Rome in an Italian aircraft carrying mostly Italian passengers. The skipper made a landing at Heathrow that was good but not outstanding, whereupon all the Italians clapped! British passengers would have grumbled at the slightest thump (and we can all make them from time to time). Then there are the inclusive tours to Israel, many of them flown by El Al. As soon as the seat-belt lights go out, everyone is out of their seat, shaking hands with complete strangers. They are not to know but a shock awaits them on arrival in the country for the first time. Israel is so small, they put notices in all the railway carriages which say, 'Passengers opening the windows are requested not to lean out over Jordan'.

Some of the airlines operating the internal routes in France employ pilots who think they are flying Mirage fighters, while most American captains seem unable to deliver any message to the passengers without including the words 'at this time'. The average British Airways skipper can be relied upon never to display the slightest emotion, whatever the situation, for example: 'Ladies and gentlemen, this is your captain speaking. Afraid there is a slight problem which may delay your arrival – the port wing has just dropped off. Thank you for flying British Airways.'

This brings me to the subject of Captain Speaking. There was a time when all communications between the crew in the sharp end of the ship and the fare-paying customers in the gin-and-tonic area was via message cards passed back down the cabin from row to row. A mate of mine, by name of Peter Hearne, was once on a business trip flying from Washington to New York when such a card landed in his lap. It said: 'Captain Sebenhauser presents his compliments and wishes to inform you that we are now cruising at 29,000 feet. Our speed is 500 mph and we shall be landing at New York at 4.30 pm. Have a good day.'

It so happens that friend Hearne had kept a card from a previous flight which, in essence, said that they would be landing at Heathrow, London, England at 9.45 pm. This he swapped for the New York one and passed back to the row of seats behind. Inside five minutes, panic erupted inside that aircraft and 138 people were demanding to get off then and there.

Now we have a public announcement system and a voice which says 'This is your captain speaking'. Because of this, there is a tendency in aviation circles to call all airline skippers Captain Speaking, but the ability to keep in touch with passengers can be a mixed blessing; certainly it must be used with discretion. For example, during the days when it was an event if the British motor industry turned out a reliable family car, a party of shopfloor workers from a well-known Coventry works chartered a large aircraft for an outing to Nice. The aircraft taxied out ready for take-off and then there was a long delay while a stream of in-coming jets landed in rapid succession. To reassure his passengers, the captain came on the announcement system and said: 'This is Captain Speaking speaking. Sorry about the delay due to heavy traffic landing at the airport. We expect to depart in five minutes. Meanwhile I can assure you that during your trip to Nice, we on the flight-deck will be doing our job as carefully and conscientiously as you do in the car factory.'

It took the cabin staff all of ten minutes to get the passengers back into their seats.

A mate of mine on a long-distance flight found himself on an Italian 747. The cabin service was good, the food was excellent, and he was actually enjoying the thought of spending several more hours in the 'aluminium tube', when the cabin-announcement system burst into life and a voice emerged thus: 'Ladies and a'gentlemen, ees a'Captain Ravioli speaking. I have a'some good news and I have a'some bad news. First I am a'going to give the bad news. We are lost! And now for the good news. We are a'making good time.'

By contrast was a captain of the old school on that famous German airline, Hansafardt, who as they were approaching the destination delivered a tirade to the fare-paying inmates which ended with the command '. . .und ven I say vassenzer zeatbelts I vant to hear – VON KLICK!'

Of course, the flight-deck crew (captain, first officer and, in some aircraft, flight engineer) are not the only ones with access to the cabin-announcement system. The chief stewards and senior stewardess often have mind-blowing information to impart: 'We will shortly be serving drinks';

—UND VEN
I SAY VASSENZER
ZEAT BELTS
I VANT TO
HEAR—
VON
KLICK!

'The duty free is now open' and of less fascination, 'The captain has now switched on the "fasten your safety belts" sign'.

On one occasion, a large jet operated by a famous British airline, in those days known as B.*.*.C, landed at Nairobi. While taxiing to the terminal building, it passed another large jet belonging to an equally famous American airline which regards itself as 'Number One' (it must be; their adverts admit the fact). The American jet had obviously burst a couple of tyres on one undercarriage leg and it was standing, forlorn and left wing down, with the offending wheels off the taxiway and on the grass. At that stage, the voice of the chief steward came over the cabin-announcement system of the B.*.*.C. aircraft: 'Ladies and gentlemen, as you all know Pan Demonium Airways advertise themselves as "The World's Most Experienced Airline". If you will kindly look out of the windows on the left of the cabin you will see them having one of their experiences.'

It so happens that, for some reason, a director of Pan Demonium Airways was travelling in the B.*.*.C. aircraft. And he didn't laugh.

Of course, the introduction of instant communications with the fare-paying clients places additional responsibilities on the shoulders of the cabin staff. They have to be very careful what they say; mistakes are all too easy to make and they can cause confusion. Like the stewardess with a particularly charming voice who told 380 passengers on a flight to New York, 'We are now cruising at 550 feet at a speed of 28,000 miles per hour.'

It is only when you have travelled the world a little that one comes to appreciate its sheer size. That old saying, 'it's a small world', is utter rubbish; ask any jaded airline crew that has just flown twelve hours non-stop from London to Johannesburg. And talking of long flights there was this delightful old lady visiting her sister in Australia for the first time in many years. She had never flown outside Europe before but since the trip was to Strineland it seemed only right and proper to her orderly mind that the experts on that part of the world were likely to be Australians and they should therefore be entrusted with flying her all those miles. So she booked on that internationally acclaimed Australian airline known as Quaintarse.

They were in the closing hours of the flight, the air was gin clear with not a cloud in sight and below, stretching in all directions and going on forever, was the Pacific. The dear old lady watched this in some awe, for truly it was a spiritually uplifting experience for those of a serious mind and a poetic disposition. One of the Aussie cabin staff walked by and in tones of mingled wonder and near disbelief the old lady exclaimed, 'Steward – just look at all that water!'

To which the man replied in accents Strine, 'Yer – I knaw laidy. An' that's only what's on top.'

Then there was the case of the other old lady who had never flown in her life. Indeed she had always promised herself that to indulge in the unnatural was to court disaster (personally I have never regarded horse riding as *natural*. If you fall out of an aeroplane, you know what to expect; if you fall off a horse, the beast will probably trample all over you and then laugh, showing those ghastly yellow teeth). However, there comes a time in life when fixed principles may have to give way to reality and, in this case, the dear old lady had a sister living in the south of France. She was very fond of her sister and now the poor lady was rather ill so, like it or not, our heroine was faced with having to fly.

At Heathrow she was assisted through baggage check-in, passport control and security before boarding a BEA (now part of British Airways) jet. After about forty minutes, she undid her safety-belt, got out of her seat and walked, looking neither left nor right, towards the rear of the aircraft, where the girls were busy getting ready to serve dinner. The old dear caught the eye of one of them, and said, 'Excuse me, but can you direct me to the ladies' powder room please.'

Of course it's boys and girls together in an aircraft, even the largest of them, but the stewardess replied, 'Afraid you have come to the wrong end of the cabin, madam, but if you turn around and walk towards the front, you will see the toilets on the left-hand side.'

So off the old lady toddled, past all the rows of seats and again looking neither left nor right until she came to a door straight ahead, which she opened. Unknown to her, she was on the flight-deck, but as this was a night flight all she could make out in the darkness was a series of fluorescent instrument dials and the outline of three peaked caps, all looking forward. So she backed out, quietly closed the door behind her and toddled back to the stewardess at the rear of the cabin. 'You'll never believe what is going on in the ladies' powder room,' she told the girl in breathless astonishment. 'You'll never believe it. There are three men in there and they are all watching television!'

A somewhat different story is that of the very smartly dressed and well-spoken city gent who burst on to the flight-deck, gun in hand, and demanded of the captain, 'Fly me to New York!'

'What the hell are you playing at?' asked the pilot. 'We *are* going to New York.'

'Thank the Lord for that,' said the city gent. 'Last three times we've been hijacked.'

YOU'LL NEVER BELIEVE WHAT IS GOING ON IN THE LADIES' POWDER ROOM... THERE ARE THREE MEN IN THERE AND THEY ARE ALL WATCHING TELEVISION!

Chapter 6
IN THE POSH END OF THE SHIP

There are airlines and airlines but, without exception, they all have one thing in common: according to the public relations people, theirs is the finest airline in the world (although in terms of cabin comforts your ancient aviation scribe is of the opinion that some of them should not be allowed to run a village bus service). The International Air Transport Association (IATA) ensures that no airline can undercut the fares of another, so the only way the more enterprising can compete is by offering free drinks and better cabin service for the same money. One Far Eastern airline, for example, uses real silver, good china and linen table-cloths in the up-market parts of the aircraft; while another, proud of the extra room allowed its passengers advertises, 'We allow plenty of room, even for passengers with six feet'.

The travel agencies are very mindful of the need to offer special service to customers booking more exclusive seats. For one winter sports tour, which included First Class air travel each way, they advertised, 'If you break a leg during one of our skiing holidays, we will give you £50 off your next winter break.'

When you book that holiday on the Costa Fortune, everything will have been done to keep the price down. Economics demand that you be packed into the aircraft virtually in one another's laps, like consenting adults. I once heard a passenger say to the chap sitting next to him, 'You breath in while I breath out.' Now the business fraternity and, even more so, government officials, might be flying in the same aircraft as us Economy Class mortals, but theirs is another world.

Their step up in travel comfort is usually given some high-powered name like Club, Super Club, Club Europe or Business Class. Passengers travelling thus sit in a separate cabin in front of the masses; they enjoy wider seats with more leg-room, better food and unlimited free champers. The pampering starts when you arrive at the airport, because there is usually a separate check-in desk for Club and First Class passengers and sometimes a member of the airline staff may walk along the queues to ensure that they are not mixed up with the bucket-and-spade fraternity. 'Are you in the Club?', to which one indignant middle-aged lady with a shrill voice replied, 'What – at my time of life!'

Even more exalted than Club is First Class and a separate luxury cabin is provided for these passengers. It is right up front, in the nose of the aircraft, on the principle that folk who have paid three times the Economy Class fare are entitled to get there before the peasants. They will also be the first to hit any mountains the crew may decide to fly into. It is all part of the aviation scene that as you move forward from the Economy to the Club cabin, the inmates wear a 'so what – we have done it all before' look on their faces. And if you walk still further towards the sharp end of the wagon, there in the First Class cabin will be a picture of utter boredom. Personally, if I had just paid £1,400 *one way* to New York (when Economy return may be bought for as little as £340), I would be anything but bored; every detail of the trip and the service would have my undivided attention.

It is well known among regular air travellers that if you want to go from any place to anywhere in the world, you go through London Heathrow. And you will be late. But as previously mentioned, having checked in for your Club or First Class flight, the major airlines will usually offer you the hospitality of a special lounge where free refreshments are poured out. Very occasionally a few of these up-market passengers have been known to become airborne before the 'plane actually leaves the ground.

Now a ritual that must take place at the start of every flight, however often the passengers may have flown before, is the demonstration given by cabin staff, explaining how to use the emergency oxygen masks and the location of the emergency exits. There was this slightly alcoholic mob, fresh out of the Club lounge at the airport, and to every piece of advice they chorused 'Here, here' and 'Rhubarb, rhubarb'.

Club Class they may have been, but enough was enough and the purser said, 'Gentlemen, Simon and Garfunkel may have written the song "Fifty ways to leave your lover" but there are only six ways out of this aircraft, so you had better shut up and take notice'.

Fortunately there are very few drunken passenger problems, but they can be a menace even in penny numbers. There was this chap in the Club cabin who was determined to get his money's worth of free booze. Trouble was he would drink but couldn't and he so terrorised one of the stewardesses that she took refuge on the flight-deck. So happens the captain on this trip was a big impressive character and he grabbed a small fire axe (carried on the flight-deck as an emergency tool), marched into the Club Class cabin, stuck the blunt end under the obnoxious passenger's chin, lifted him out of the seat with one hand, glared at him and said, 'Any more trouble and I will eat you!' That passenger was taken suddenly sober.

Another well-known source of trouble on the airlines was a famous comedian who stood less than five feet tall (no *not*

SOME PASSENGERS HAVE BEEN KNOWN TO BECOME AIRBORNE BEFORE THE PLANE ACTUALLY LEAVES THE GROUND.

the late Arthur Askey). He was a nice enough chap until there were a few drinks in him. Then he would pinch the stewardesses' bottoms and make lewd suggestions. On one flight, with the free drinks in Club Class inside him, he groped one of the girls as she walked past and said, 'Hallo gorgeous. What would you say to a little f**k?'

He had picked one of the more experienced cabin staff and she looked him in the eye and replied, 'Hallo little f**k.'

In the days before jets, when long journeys entailed a number of refuelling stops, there was this First Class passenger who had drunk rather a lot in the VIP lounge before boarding the plane. As a result, by the time they had started the engines, pushed back from the parking ramp, taxied out, taken off and got into the climb, he was sitting legs crossed and bursting to spend a penny. He called the steward and said, 'Where is the toilet?'

'Port side,' he was told.

'My Gawd,' said the passenger, crossing his legs the other way, 'don't we land first at Gibraltar?'

Of course, not all Club and First Class passengers get themselves Brahms and Liszt in the VIP lounge before clambering aboard – far from it. Many of these worthies are hard-working citizens holding responsible positions; that is why they can afford to travel Club or First Class. There was this big shot in the City who had a series of very important appointments in New York and, being a professional to his fingertips, he had allowed himself plenty of time for the drive around the M25 to Heathrow.

Now the M25, which circles London, was inadequate before they completed the last piece of the hoop and our City gent sat fuming in his silver Jaguar as one traffic hold-up after another gradually eroded the extra time he had allowed for the journey. Then he ran into fog, so on went his headlights and by the time he had arrived at the long-term car-park, jumped into the airport bus, checked in at the desk and ran towards the aircraft, a 'Where are you Mr City Gent?' was being called over the public-announcement system. He arrived just before they closed the cabin door and pushed back from the parking ramp.

He was sweating and out of breath as a stewardess led him to his seat, but now he could wind down and look forward to his six days in New York, where he had many friends. Sitting next to him in the window seat was a charming old lady who had never flown before. They took off, the jet nosed up into the climb like a homesick angel and the old dear, eyes focused out of the window, became a girl of 18 again as an excited running commentary poured forth: 'Look! isn't it wonderful? You can see everything so clearly, like little toys on the ground. And Oh look! There is the car-park. Can you see? There's a silver Jaguar parked down there with its headlights on.'

Cabin safety announcements recited as a matter of ritual can have their hidden dangers, an example being the loss of passenger confidence that followed a detailed run-down on lifeboat drill during one of the London to Manchester shuttle flights. 'Who on earth wants to hear all that on a flight such as this?' demanded one Club Class passenger, to which a charming stewardess responded, 'Perhaps it is because of the Manchester Ship Canal.'

For a short while, one British airline provided Club Class passengers with an attractive secretary who worked in a little office at one end of the cabin. Business men had to pay for her services (as a shorthand typist, of course) but the experiment was not a success.

In my experience, the food is better in Club than in

LOOK! ISN'T IT WONDERFUL? YOU CAN SEE EVERYTHING SO CLEARLY, LIKE LITTLE TOYS ON THE GROUND. AND OH LOOK! THERE IS THE CAR PARK. CAN YOU SEE? THERE'S A SILVER JAGUAR PARKED DOWN THERE WITH ITS HEAD LIGHTS ON!

Economy Class – and so it should be having regard to the difference in price. However, this is by no means universal and there is one American airline in my experience that has a reputation for dreadful catering in all parts of the aeroplane. On one occasion, the chief stewardess in the Club Class cabin told the inmates, 'Ladies and gentlemen, you may have noticed there are three entrées on the menu tonight. Please don't be disappointed if, by the time the food trolley reaches you, the one you have chosen has all gone. I can assure you they all taste the same.'

One of the perks sometimes handed out to First Class and Club passengers is a nice, refreshing little hot towel. One mystified customer, who had obviously not come across this before, stared at it for half a minute, then cleaned the adjacent window with it.

Then there are the demanding passengers who spend the entire flight pressing the stewardess bell. One mature lady of the old school, who was used to being pampered and having her own way, told the senior steward she wished to visit the flight-deck as she had an important question to ask the captain. So the steward went up to the centre of all aeronautical learning and said, 'We've got a right one here skipper and she says it's urgent.' Well, it was a night flight, air-traffic control had been messing him about and the captain was in no mood for a difficult lady passenger, but she was in First Class so he had better put on his gentleman pilot act (there are a few of us around).

The lady was ushered on to the flight-deck and after polite introductions she said, 'Captain, I am concerned to know how you are able to find your way in this dark.'

'Well, it's all very simple really,' replied the skipper with a straight face. 'If you look out of the left window, you will see a red light on our wing-tip. And if you look at the right wing-tip, there is a green light. All I have to do is fly down the middle.'

So important is the Club and First Class traveller to the airlines of the world that a number of specialist magazines are published for their needs. The British magazine, *Executive Travel*, often reports the most remarkable goings-on. There was the First Class passenger travelling from Florida to California who asked how long the journey usually took. The stewardess replied, 'I don't know; we haven't made it yet.'

On another occasion, the charming stewardess on a well-known Eastern airline advised the passengers, '. . . not to be alarmed by the steam pouring out of the ventilation slots in the cabin. This is a characteristic of the air-conditioning system and if anything were to go seriously wrong I would be the first to let you know as I left the aircraft.'

One of the less attractive features of all modes of travel is the ship, train or jet that leaves late. One long-suffering Business Class passenger on a Pan Demonium Airways flight from New York to Bombay was so delighted when the plane left on time that he sent for the chief steward and congratulated him. Rather frostily the man admitted, 'Actually, sir, this is yesterday's flight.'

Of a different nature was the lengthy delay at Guangzhou in China. After almost seven hours, a Chinese airline official announced, 'So sorry; aircraft sick. Will find another aircraft.' Another two hours went by, then the same official announced, 'Second aircraft more sick than first one. So will take first one.'

Then there are those fortunately rare occasions when the baggage arrives at a totally different destination to that of its owner. One regular Business Class passenger suffered a number of such experiences, so he wrote to the airline concerned complaining that 'my luggage seems to have done more travelling than me this last year'. While on the subject, I am advised that on one occasion Lady Harlech arrived at the desk of a well-known airline and said to the check-in clerk, 'Although I am flying to Rome, I would like that bag sent to Istanbul, that one to Delhi and the big one over there to Sydney.'

The check-in clerk was naturally taken aback and replied, 'Sorry madam, we are not allowed to do that because your baggage must travel with you.'

'I cannot imagine why,' retorted Lady Harlech, 'You did it last time and I hadn't even asked!'

Another airline 'nasty', one that is fortunately less common these days, is overbooking; as an insurance against passengers who without warning fail to show up (and who can nevertheless claim a full refund on the fare), some carriers deliberately sell more tickets than there are seats in the aircraft. They seem prepared to face the music when irate customers checking in are told: 'Sorry; there has been a mix-up but we will try and get you on another flight. How are you fixed for Thursday (this being Tuesday)?'

A world famous American airline once made the genuine mistake of double-booking an entire Boeing 747 – yes all 400 seats of it! But in Nigeria, when one of the local flights was over-booked by a factor of three, the local military sorted the problem by making the passengers run twice around the aircraft. The winners got the seats.

Things happen in Third World countries that may be normal to the locals but that are certain to raise the eyebrows of Western passengers booked into the plush areas of the plane. There was this jet belonging to an Eastern airline that was about to depart from Bangladesh

ALTHOUGH I AM FLYING TO ROME, I WOULD LIKE THAT BAG SENT TO ISTANBUL, THAT ONE TO DELHI AND THE BIG ONE OVER THERE TO SYDNEY.
SORRY MADAME, YOUR BAGGAGE MUST TRAVEL WITH YOU.
I CANNOT IMAGINE WHY, YOU DID IT LAST TIME AND I HADN'T EVEN ASKED!

for Heathrow. The baggage was on, the customers were all tied into their seats and the time for departure came and went. There was a loud banging on the entrance door at the front of the cabin and a lot of muffled shouting. The cabin staff opened it to reveal a near hysterical figure standing outside. It was the captain of the aircraft trying to get in.

Of course, most folk who travel Club or First Class are either on company business or they have made it to the point where paying for the ticket does not make them ill. As such, they should be regarded as the real international jet setters. However, I must tell you that newcomers to the 'international' world are in for a few surprises. For one thing, it is quite astonishing how much English is spoken by foreigners (if there is such an animal among us 'internationals'). The Swedes, for example, speak it at least as well as the English and probably converse in American better than most Americans.

There may be lots of jet setters who speak excellent English, but it was only after seeing something I had written translated into Swedish that it brought home to me how a word may be perfectly well mannered in one language but quite unmentionable in decent company when used in another tongue. I asked a Swedish friend of mine, by name of Bo (all Swedish males are called Bo), why it was that the vulgar word 'fart' appeared repeatedly in the translation of something perfectly gentlemanly I had written. He assured me that, in Swedish, the word means speed. He went on to say that at one time there was a very successful Swedish motor magazine named *Fart*. Just imagine being a journalist working for that magazine and having to present your card at a motor show ('Please tell Mr Jones that Bo Svegensen of *Fart* wishes to see him').

The dreadful word impinges on Swedish aviation too. As something of a photographer, I naturally know about light meters and all readers of this little book will have a more or less daily relationship with parking meters and gas or electric meters. But when I asked my friend Bo what the Swedish name was for that essential instrument on the flight-deck, the air-speed indicator, he said it was a *fartmeter*! The mind boggles!

The nationalised airline run jointly by Sweden, Norway and Denmark is called SAS, which stands for Scandinavian Airlines System. When one of their pilots is in a hurry to make up for that late departure, he opens up the power in order to fly at maximum *fart*. But when flying near the airport prior to landing, he must naturally adopt a low *fart* (and surely that is better out than in, as they say in the classics). I suppose it is not uncommon for Swedish business men to complain bitterly of being stopped by the police for *farting* on the way home from the airport.

It is a constant source of wonder to me how many newcomers to air travel seem to have a morbid interest in sanitation. 'What happens to "it" – does the captain have a notice in the cockpit reminding him not to pull the main flush while flying over Reigate or some other plush area?' Well there ain't no main flush and there is no hole in the bottom of the aircraft; the rate payers would not allow such an arrangement. Instead, it is all neutralised very effectively with chemicals and emptied at the destination, where they have purpose-built vehicles with big flexible tubes that plug into the places provided for emptying the sewage.

Having explained the plumbing, it is perhaps opportune to add that you must never – but *never* – smoke in the loos, not even in the First Class. In the 'little rooms' are paper towels, free tissues and the usual rolls of paper. A stray cigarette end might start an uncontrollable fire in a confined space and that could prove catastrophic. Understandably, a 'no smoking in the petty' announcement is always made before take-off and the cabin staff are ever on the look-out for those among us who, for their own warped reasons, cannot be told.

On one quite long flight, a large gentleman in the First Class cabin wandered down towards the toilets with a smoking cigar in his hand. 'Sorry sir, but you are not allowed to smoke in the toilets,' said an attractive young stewardess, whereupon the large-size gent extinguished his cigar with a display of obvious displeasure.

Several hours later, the same passenger again wandered down the aisle, obviously making for the toilets, with a smouldering cigar in one hand. The same stewardess reminded him once more about not smoking in the loo and there was another show of impatience as he reluctantly extinguished his expensive smoke. When, shortly before landing, he drifted cigar in hand towards the plumbing for a third time, the stewardess felt she should handle this obviously very difficult passenger with more tact. 'Would you like me to hold it for you?' she enquired with a charming smile.

As the late Eric Morecambe would have said, there is no answer to that.

Chapter 7

OVERHEARD ON THE RADIO

There are still many of us around who remember the days when only the largest aircraft had a radio and even those communicated by Morse code. Then radio-telephony came along and, although the early equipment was so weak you might just as well have opened the window and shouted to the chaps on the ground, when VHF arrived (Very High Frequency radio-telephony was pioneered during the war by the RAF), communications between air and ground became a practical proposition.

There are always those among us who resent progress and as more and more radio became available, the deadbeats could be heard moaning about black boxes being fitted in aircraft so that someone on the ground could tell the pilots what to do at a time when they did not want to do it. However, apart from the obvious practical advantages of being able to call up the destination and be told in response to a weather enquiry, 'It's pissing with rain down here', some entertaining things can be heard over the aircraft radio bands from time to time.

During World War 2, when security was vital, airfields were never referred to over the radio by their proper names. Instead they were given call-signs that were changed at intervals to fox the enemy. One station was allocated the call-sign 'Duplex Tower', a name that any idiot could have told them was asking for trouble, particularly since many of the flying control staff were WAAFs (female airmen). So this wag takes off on his way to some other RAF station, presses the transmit button and says, 'Durex Tower, Able Charlie two six, airborne and on course, over.'

To which a bored WAAF voice replied, 'Able Charlie two six, the call-sign is Duplex Tower, *not* Durex Tower. This is flying control, not birth control.'

Naturally, the boys in blue who had learned special skills in the RAF were not slow to capitalise on their asset and unless there was a profession or a special job awaiting them, it was a case of carry on as usual in civvie street. Thus, many of the RAF pilots went into the airlines. There was this ex-bomber boy who had flown a couple of tours of operations in Lancasters, mostly over Germany. After joining what was then called British European Airways, he took a load of passengers to Frankfurt, but after landing he was not entirely sure about how he should taxi to the passenger terminal. First he turned left, then he turned right and finally he stopped on the runway. The voice of an exasperated German air-traffic controller came over the radio, 'Bealine (the airline's call-sign) two four zero. Vat are you doing? Heff you not been here before?'

To which the ex-bomber pilot replied, 'Yes, I was here during the war but I didn't stop.'

The air-traffic control system is really quite remarkable. Departing and in-coming aircraft are sequenced to ensure safe and orderly use of the runways of the world. When the weather is good, life is so easy it's a shame to take the money, but poor weather slows the landing rate. Since an airliner cannot stop, like a train, there are radio beacons at strategic places around the major airports, around which aircraft can fly a race-track pattern while they await their turn to land. On a busy day, air-traffic control may instruct a number of aircraft to fly around the same beacon at 1,000-foot height intervals. This is known as flying a 'hold' and a number of aircraft flogging around a beacon at different

DUREX TOWER, ABLE CHARLIE TWO SIX, AIRBORNE AND ON COURSE, OVER.
ABLE CHARLIE TWO SIX, THE CALL-SIGN IS DUPLEX TOWER, NOT DUREX TOWER. THIS IS FLYING CONTROL, NOT BIRTH CONTROL.

levels are known as a 'stack'.

On the occasion I have in mind, a BO Airways jumbo had flown across the Atlantic and the weather was perfect until they entered the London area, where visibility was so bad even the birds were walking. So the skipper was told to do a hold on the Epsom beacon (so called because that is where they have built it).

After about twenty minutes in the stack, Heathrow gave the captain permission to leave the beacon and point in the general direction of the runway so that he might land. The visibility was still poor and the skipper had his head down, eyes glued to twitching needles, ears awaiting various aviation-type sounds that would announce his proximity to the runway threshold. Suddenly, the senior steward burst on to the flight-deck, tapped the captain on the shoulder and in some agitation said, 'Skipper, skipper –'

'What do you want, bothering me at a time like this?' growled the captain as the ground got nearer and nearer.

'We've got an old lady who seems to be locked in one of the toilets and she can't get out,' explained the steward.

Now company rules are loud and clear about landing with customers in the loo. It is simply not allowed. So, in something of a rage, the captain pressed his transmit button and said, 'London Approach, I am breaking off the landing because we have one old lady locked in the lavatory.'

To which the controller replied, 'Roger. You may hold on the Epsom beacon from Monday to Saturday.'

Although the Met man would have us believe they have the weather situation in hand, they are always glad to receive actual reports from pilots in flight. There was this French chap, I shall call him Pierre, who had just crossed the Channel on his way to Gatwick. 'What is your present weather?' enquired the Gatwick controller.

'In and out of ze base of cloud,' replied Pierre.

Unfortunately neither Pierre's English accent nor the radio in his aircraft were very good and the chap at Gatwick was unable to understand. So, using standard aviation terminology, he said, 'Say again please.'

'In and out of ze base of cloud,' repeated Pierre.

Again the Gatwick controller was unable to understand, so when he asked a second time for the message to be repeated, an irate Pierre pressed the button and shouted, 'In and out of ze bottom.'

In another aircraft flying at 30,000 feet, someone pressed the button and a hysterical voice said, '*vive le sport.*'

From time to time one hears some pretty choice radio chat while aircraft are manoeuvring on the ground, particularly at big airports where the first twenty minutes of the flight may be spent taxiing from the terminal building to the runway. One hot, smoggy day at J. F. Kennedy Airport, New York, a long stream of jets was making its way towards the holding point from where, one by one, they would be given permission by air-traffic control to taxi on to the runway and take off. There had been a number of delays and the oppressive weather was not exactly easing the tension in the air. There was an edge in the voice of the controller as he spoke to the pilots on the 'Tower' frequency and the replies he was getting back from the various captains were frigid, formal and tinged with irritation.

Just as the long caravan of jets arrived at the holding point, it was decided to change the duty runway because some pilots had been complaining that the low, hazy sun was blinding them during take-off. So the controller came on the air and told all aircraft now at the holding point to taxi another three miles to the next runway. It was the last straw and one of the skippers registered his protest by pressing the transmit button and saying 'Oh s**t'. The controller was affronted; he had never heard such language over the radio before and, in obvious anger, he demanded to know 'Who said s**t on my frequency?' That did it. One after another, ten or more airline captains in turn pressed their buttons and in mock protest said, 'I didn't say s**t on your frequency,' 'I didn't,' etc. etc.

Another function of the air-traffic control service is to prevent aircraft flying into one another, so each flight is carefully planned and the details are passed to the pilot in the form of a 'clearance'. Without delving into the complexities of the various rules, I should perhaps mention that when a pilot flies from A to B in sight of the ground and under his own navigation, he is said to be operating under Visual Flight Rules, known in the trade as VFR.

A mate of mine, who until his retirement was a senior skipper with a leading British airline, was one day in command of an aircraft flying from London to Paris. There had been a minor technical fault which caused a forty-five minute delay. That put him in the rush-hour at Heathrow and, as a result, he had to queue for another twenty minutes before they let him on to the runway. Just as he was about to open the taps and take off, the Heathrow controller called him on the radio and said, 'Bealine two four zero (my mate's call-sign) delay your take-off. There are three swans at the end of the runway.'

That did it. He was already more than an hour behind schedule and this was the last straw.

'And what kind of bloody clearance have they got?' enquired my exasperated friend.

'VFR to Windsor Park,' came the immediate reply.

As if VFR was not enough to contend with, the actual weather conditions that allow such flights are known as VMC, which stands for Visual Meteorological Conditions. Because some letters sound pretty much the same when spoken over the radio, or even a telephone, an international agreed phonetic alphabet is used. Thus VMC, when spoken over the radio, becomes Victor Mike Charlie.

There were a couple of likely lads, in fact brothers from up north, who had made a bit of brass and invested in a light plane. They would go up at weekends and tootle around the local area, nothing ambitious, just a little jolly to view from above what was hard to like from the ground. On the occasion I have in mind, the weather was turning nasty, so they called up the Manchester controller. Now these air-traffic controllers often have a talent for spotting tension in the air by the tone of voice being received and, by the way the radio was being used, it was obvious he was dealing with an amateur. Wishing to keep the private owner out of trouble, he naturally wanted to know what weather conditions were being experienced, so he pressed his button and enquired, 'Are you Victor Mike Charlie?', which brought the response. 'No; we are Bill and Alf Modley from Wakefield.'

Some years ago, my wife and I were partaking of a light plane air rally to West Africa. On the way south, I was taking off from Marrakesh Airport when, out of the corner of my eye, I became aware of a large dog running towards the runway. Fortunately, it sat down on the edge of the concrete and just watched me roar past and lift off. Now to hit an animal while taking off is not funny (it wipes the smile off the dog's face too), so I pressed the transmit button and said, 'Marrakesh Tower there is a large dog sitting on the edge of your runway.'

'What colour ees eet,' asked the Moroccan controller.

'Mostly black,' I replied.

'Black one ees OK,' I was assured by the controller.

I later learned that this particular dog belonged to the airport manager and it simply loved to watch the planes taking off. Well, there is no harm in that.

Not long after President Reagan took office, the American

ARE YOU VICTOR MIKE CHARLIE?
NO; WE ARE BILL AND ALF MODLEY FROM WAKEFIELD.

air-traffic controllers' union called all its members out on strike. The President sacked the lot and only about half of them were taken back. Some are of the opinion that there were too many controllers before the punch-up, but, while the drama was being enacted, down in Texas they put some of the stewardesses in the tower. Those readers who have visited my favourite state will know that the locals never refer to a person as 'you'. It is always 'you all' (pronounced yo'all).

At one particularly busy downtown airfield, where they handle a lot of regional air traffic, things can get more than a little animated because there is only one east-west runway. During the strike, an American Airlines aircraft called up for landing instructions and one of these delightful Southern Belles replied, 'Ah hear you honey. Yo'all can land to the east.'

Five minutes later, there was a call for landing instructions from a Continental Airlines skipper, which provoked the reply, 'Hi there Continental. Yo'all can land to the west.'

Now the first captain heard this, swallowed hard, then pressed the button and said, 'Hey, what gives down there? You've got us both landing in opposite directions on the same runway!'

To which Honey Child replied, 'Now yo'all take care up there.'

Among British civil aircraft to have enjoyed considerable success in the immediate post-war years was the Bristol Freighter. It was a bold concept in its day because one version of it was designed to accommodate three medium- or two large-size cars. Several airlines did a roaring trade on the cross-Channel routes and it was a common sight at some airports to see cars being driven on and off through massive clam-shell doors built into the noses of the aircraft.

By modern standards, the Freighter was not a very large aircraft but, to accommodate the cars and their passengers, it had a very deep and boxy fuselage with slab sides. Even its best friends could not describe it as a pretty bird; in fact it was rather akin to a flying version of the Imperial War Museum. It was during a sales tour of the United States that one of these winged elephants landed at Chicago. The duty controller in the tower did a double-take, reached for his binoculars, then pressed the transmit button and said over the radio, 'Hell man – what's that!'

To which the very stiff upper lip demonstration pilot from Weybridge answered, 'We are a Bristol Freighter.'

'Make it yourself?' asked the American controller.

Inexperienced pilots do, at times, get lost, but the air-traffic control service can usually locate them on radar or by other means. Lost sheep are then steered towards an airfield, but the controller must be sure there is enough fuel to get them there. So among the questions likely to be asked by the helping hand on the ground is 'What is your endurance?' On one occasion the poor lost ace of the air replied, 'I'm not sure, but it's either the Sun Life or the Prudential.'

Then there is the tale of the inexperienced private pilot who was quite good when the weather was kind but not so hot at instrument flying. One day, when the weather should have made him stop at home and read a book, he went to the local club, took off in his favourite plane, rapidy found himself in never-ending dirty grey cloud and got himself thoroughly lost. Now this little drama was being enacted on the edge of the London Terminal Area – a vast chunk of sky that is reserved for suitably qualified pilots flying on an instrument flight plan. Fortunately, the area is covered by a first-class radar service, known as London Radar. So there was this long, drawn-out chat over the radio while the private pilot was steered away from trouble, something the radar controller on the ground

could have done without because the skies of London are like 'Red Indian Country' – thick with aircraft.

By a piece of excellent radar vectoring, all of it delivered in a calm, courteous voice, our inexperienced friend was safely lowered over the Thames until he broke cloud, heading away from trouble. By now determined not to lose himself again, he is up there with a large scale AA map of London, ticking off the streets as he flies past.

'Are you now certain of your position?' enquired the weary radar controller.

'Yes indeed – I am now passing Blackwater,' came the reply.

'Well, you are advised to see a doctor,' said the disenchanted controller.

Aircraft approaching their destinations must take a prescribed route to the airport; they cannot be allowed to descend on it from all directions because that could lead to a second Battle of Britain. Aircraft are cleared, by the airways controllers, from one radio beacon to the next. And they are allowed to descend as they get nearer and nearer the destination. For the last seventy miles or so, the 300-ton jet that has flown you home on the power of a QE2-size liner will be throttled right back, actually becoming a massive glider.

The radio beacons are named after their location – Seaford, Bovingdon, Biggin Hill, for example – and so that pilots may reassure themselves they are not homing in on BBC2 or Capital Radio, an identification is at intervals transmitted in Morse. Biggin Hill, for example, sends out the signal 'Big'. Now, as previously mentioned, some letters sound the same when heard over the telephone (Bs, Gs and Ds can easily be confused), so in 'radio speak' the Biggin Hill beacon (identification letters BH) would become 'the Bravo Hotel beacon'.

There was this British Airways 747 aiming for a major Indian airport and the skipper let it be known he was expecting to reach their airspace boundary in twenty minutes, to which the Indian controller replied, 'Roger, you are cleared over the Bravo Alpha beacon at 2,500 feet.'

Five minutes later, the captain of a Lufthansa jet

contacted the same controller and said he was due to arrive at about the same time as the British Airways flight.

'Roger,' acknowledged the Indian voice, 'you too are cleared over the Bravo Alpha beacon at 2,500 feet.'

Now the British Airways captain heard this in disbelief. So he pressed the button and protested, 'What goes on down there? You've just cleared two jumbos over the same beacon at the same height!'

There was an embarrassed pause, then the controller said, 'Oh goodness gracious – looks like being another day like yesterday.'

In some airlines, particularly B*****h A*****s, captains enjoy a status that is only equalled by a High Court judge. This B*****h A*****s jumbo jet was in the closing stages of a flight from New York to London. It had already been allowed to descend from 30,000 to 20,000 feet, but Heathrow was coming nearer and nearer. The captain wished to avoid a last-minute steep descent, so he turned to his first officer and said, 'Tell London we want to descend to 13,000 feet.'

The first officer did as commanded, but the London Airways controller would not cooperate and he replied, 'Negative (aviation speak for 'no'), hold your present altitude.'

Now the captain heard the reply and he was very displeased. 'I'll see to this,' he said grimly as he pressed the button and announced, 'London Airways, this is the captain speaking; I wish to descend immediately to 13,000 feet.'

To which the chap on the ground replied, 'Roger, captain, you may descend to 13,000 feet, but leave your aircraft where it is.'

Chapter 8

IRISH DEPARTMENT

The Americans tell Polish stories and in Brazil they tell Portuguese jokes. French people tell Belgian stories and the Swedes tell them about the Norwegians; that is until the Norwegians found oil and the Swedes, refusing to take their neighbours seriously, refused to come in on the deal. Now the Norwegians tell Swedish stories.

In Britain (England in particular) we tell Irish stories. And what would we do without them. All this folklore about the Irish being as thick as two planks is something the Irish invented for the English. Indeed, they will tell you with a perfectly straight face that God made the Irish simple so the English could understand them. So you must take this chapter with a large pinch of salt, preferably washed down by a pint of Guinness.

A lot of people do not realise how many citizens of neutral Ireland joined the British forces during World War 2. For instance, there was this Lancaster pilot from Limerick who had a flight engineer from Cork in his crew. The pilot was a Roman Catholic, his flight engineer was a Protestant and they used to argue like merry hell – in the air and on the ground. They were on a raid over Germany, fires were burning on the ground as far as the eye could see and shells were bursting around the aircraft, some of them so close you could smell the cordite. All this did nothing to stop the Irishmen arguing among themselves until one shell put a hole through the left wing. At that point the pilot turned to his fellow countryman and said, 'Well one ting, Paddy, we can at least tank de Valera for keeping us out of dis bloody war.'

Having a go at the Irish does not stop at the citizens of the Emerald Isle; there are even jokes about their wildlife and animals. Like the Irish woodworm that was found dead in a brick and the Irish dog that used to chase parked cars. However, this book is devoted to aviation, so I must first tell you about the two Irish caterpillars walking side by side along the edge of a lane. Suddenly a butterfly flew overhead and one caterpillar turned to the other and said, 'Mother of God! You'll never get me up in one of those.'

In my own experience I have always found the Irish very ready to please, a little too ready at times as I recall during a dance held at our nearby RAF Officers' Mess. One of the guests went up to the band and said, 'Can you do something Irish?' So they all got up from the bandstand, went outside and dug up the car-park.

Returning to the subject of flying, there was this young Irish chap who walked into the very large offices at the bottom of Regent Street, London, where BO Airways hold court. It is always a busy place, but on this occasion the world was on the move and it was like a betting shop on Derby Day. The lad went up to a girl behind the counter. Although she had a telephone clamped to each ear and her eyes were glued to a computer screen, all this was above the head of the young fellow.

'Excuse me, miss,' he said politely touching his cap, 'will you be telling me, how long does it take to fly the Atlantic?'

'Just a minute,' replied the very harassed girl, looking up for a split second.

'Thank you very much,' said the Irish boy as he turned around and walked out.

By and large, the British airlines have been remarkably free of hijacking attempts, but there was the case of a wild-eyed young Irish chap who burst on to the flight-deck, holding a

MOTHER OF GOD! YOU'LL NEVER GET ME UP IN ONE OF THOSE.

gun, and announced, 'Hold it right der; dis is a cock-up.'

Whereupon the captain and his first officer burst out laughing. 'Surely you mean "this is a hold-up"?' replied the captain.

'No, it's a cock-up,' insisted the young man. 'There are no bullets for the gun and I'm on the wrong bloody plane.'

As a matter of fact that young chap almost never made the plane. These days all passengers must go through a security check and, although he had hidden the gun in a quite ingenious manner, he was nevertheless nervous. So shifty and ill at ease was he that one of the security staff became suspicious and said, 'Can you identify yourself?'

The Irish lad borrowed a mirror from one of the women officers, took a quick look at it, then turned to the security officer and said, 'Dat's me for sure.'

Like most nations, the Irish have their own airline, and a very good one it is too. Air Fungus (the name was changed some years ago from the original Air Linctus) is a small but well-run outfit, and they even operate 747s. Like them or not, Boeing 747s, popularly known as jumbo jets, have made possible relatively cheap air tickets. Many readers will know that, in these enormous aircraft, there is an upstairs cabin reached via a small spiral staircase. Long before the first 747 flew, Boeing had a mock-up of the cabin, all very realistic but made of plywood, and to entice potential airline customers the upstairs cabin was all done up like a Darryl F. Zanuck film set. Rumour has it that when the directors of Air Fungus saw this for the first time, they gasped in utter astonishment, took several deep breaths, then in a horse whisper one of them said, 'Hail Mary! We'll never let the Protestants up here.'

All airlines have their own liveries, some more attractive than others. Air Fungus paint the top half of their aircraft

HOLD IT RIGHT DER; DIS IS A COCK-UP.
SURELY YOU MEAN "THIS IS A HOLD-UP"?
NO, IT'S A COCK-UP. THERE ARE NO BULLETS FOR THE GUN AND I'M ON THE WRONG BLOODY PLANE.

emerald green (what else), and very good it looks too. On one occasion BO Airways was short of a large aircraft, so they leased an Air Fungus Boeing 747 for a week. When the time came to return the jumbo jet, one of the BO Airways crew stuck a note on the captain's control wheel which said, 'Fly green side up.'

It was during those days of airline captains sending written messages to the passengers that another friend of mine asked a steward to give his card to the skipper of an Air Fungus jet. On it he had written 'Dear Captain, can you please tell us our present position'. A few moments later it came back with the words 'Haven't a clue. I have never been so far off course before.' That Air Fungus captain was lumbered with a very jealous wife. If she couldn't find any blonde hairs on his uniform jacket, he would be accused of having an affair with a bald stewardess.

There are some parts of the world where airliners have to depart from the airways system. Separation from other aircraft is then handled by ground-based radar. If another aircraft, identity unknown, appears to be on a converging course, the airliner will be told to look out for 'unknown traffic' and so that the flight-deck crew know where to look, the controller uses a simple procedure known as the clock code: 12 o'clock is directly ahead of the nose, 3 o'clock is on the right wing-tip, 9 o'clock is on the left; 45° to the right of the nose would be expressed as 2 o'clock, etc.

This Air Fungus plane was under radar control when the chap on the ground came up on the radio with the words, 'Air Fungus flight two six four, there is unknown traffic in your 11 o'clock position.'

'Will you be giving us another clue?' replied the Irish skipper. 'We've all got digital watches up here.'

Talking about time reminds me of the ritual among airline

crews of calling the tower on the radio before start-up and requesting a 'time check'. Obviously it is a good idea to ensure that all watches agree, particularly now that modern jets cover a mile every six-and-a-half seconds (Concorde does it in 2.8 seconds, by the way). There was this Air Fungus Boeing 747 standing on the ramp at J. F. Kennedy Airport, New York. The skipper was about to start engines for the return flight to Dublin and in fluent Emerald Isle he requested a time check over the radio.

'What airline are you?' requested the American in the tower.

'What difference does that make?' enquired the Irish captain.

'Well if you are Pan Am, the answer is thirteen hundred hours,' replied the controller. 'If you are British Airways, the time is one o'clock. And if you are Air Fungus, the big hand is on Noddy and the little hand is pointing to Big Ears.'

In a book of this kind one must, of necessity, simplify the technical bits. This I have tried to do, but it would be misleading if readers were to imagine that every aircraft produces a nice, bright and clear echo on the radar operator's screen. Sometimes heavy rain can cause echoes that threaten to swamp those of the aircraft. So some years ago they started fitting in aircraft a device based on a wartime RAF gadget. It is called a transponder and, in effect, it sits in the aircraft doing nothing in particular until a radar sweep, directed from the ground station, smites the aircraft. Then it wakes up and sends back an amplified echo.

Its talents do not end there because this clever little black box has a thing like a car mileometer on which the pilot may set a four-figure number which will appear on the radar screen alongside his echo. So not only does he appear on the screen 'loud and clear' but the aircraft is positively identified and not in danger of being mistaken by the radar controller for some other aircraft.

On the day I have in mind, this Air Fungus jet had crossed the Atlantic and was descending towards New York. Now the skies around the Big Apple are like those above any other major crossroad of the air. Radar screens are festooned with little echoes moving in all directions; it is like Piccadilly Circus in the rush-hour. Air traffic was particularly heavy that day and to provide the twitching radar controller with a little light entertainment, it so happened that the transponder in the Irish jet had gone on strike. So it was no use asking him to set up a four-figure number because it would not have appeared on the screen. Which of the many moving echoes on the screen was Air Fungus flight 244 from Dublin to New York, the controller asked himself. It would help him identify AF244 if he knew what course the captain was steering. So he pressed the transmit button and said, 'Air Fungus two four four, what course are you on?'

To which came the captain's astonishing reply, 'Will you be after standing by while I enquire.'

There was a two-minute pause while the American radar controller impatiently bit his nails, then the Irish skipper came on the air with, 'Are you there? They're just serving the prunes and custard.'

People who have never flown before are usually astonished to discover that there is hardly any sensation of height and very little impression of speed in an airliner, except perhaps while bursting through cloud into the clear blue sky above. Then a sea of brilliant white cotton wool races below the wings, appearing to become slower and slower as the aircraft climbs to its cruising level. When flying in cloud, there is no sensation of movement at all, particularly when the cloud is of a kind that produces no turbulence. It was while flying under such weather conditions on the

AIR FUNGUS TWO FOUR FOUR, WHAT COURSE ARE YOU ON?
THEY'RE JUST SERVING THE PRUNES AND CUSTARD.

Middle East routes that an old friend of mine, by name of Captain John Varley, did his PR act and walked through the cabin, chatting up the customers. His eyes latched on to a pair of young women anxiously looking at their watches.

'What time will we be landing at Cairo?' one of them asked him in a Dublin accent.

'Bang on schedule – eleven thirty,' replied the senior skipper.

'Well, if we are due there at eleven thirty,' said the other Irish girl, 'what are we doing stopped up here?'

It goes without saying that to be an air-traffic controller one must be fluent of speech and able to give an immediate response over the radio when the situation demands. With these thoughts in mind, I am reminded of a well-known aviation personality who was flying from Heathrow to Dublin. In the seat next to him was a young chap with freckles and hair that stood on end. Wishing to be sociable, the man-of-the-world enquired, 'Are you going to Dublin on holiday?'

To which the young chap replied, 'Ner–ner–ner–no; I'm her–her–having an inter–er–er view fer–fer–for a jer–jer–job as an air ter–ter–traffic ker–ker–controller', at which stage the older man was sorry he had asked.

On the return flight, he found himself sitting next to the same young chap, so he said, 'Well how did you get on? Did they give you the job?'

'It was all a ber–ber–big ker–ker–con,' the young fellow replied. 'You've ger–ger–got to be a Rer–rer–Roman Ker–ker–Catholic.'

Pilots of incoming aircraft naturally want to know what kind of weather they will have to face during the landing. So among other vital statistics, the approach controller will advise over the radio such topics as wind strength and direction, visibility, cloud base and the amount of cloud in eighths. Thus two-eighths means a quarter of the sky is obscured, four-eighths is half and eight-eighths indicates that there is complete cloud cover.

The pilot of a company executive jet was flying into an Irish airfield and when he came to the airfield weather bit, the controller reported 'Nine-eighths cloud at 1,000 feet.'

'Nine-eighths cloud!' exploded the pilot. 'I've never heard of such a thing.'

'Oh we often have eight-eighths cloud here,' replied the chap on the ground, 'but this is much worse than that.'

At the same airfield, a passenger aircraft on an internal flight landed faster than recommended; the pilot was rapidly running out of runway, so he stamped on the brakes with the enthusiastic assistance of the co-pilot, who also stood on his. As a result, the tyres deposited several pounds of rubber on the runway and one of the brakes caught fire, a rare but not unknown occurrence. All the passengers got out in an orderly manner and the airport fire-engine soon had the minor panic under control. However, the local newspaper later reported that 'Efforts to put out the fire were hampered by torrential rain.'

I am often asked why some airliners have two engines, some have three and others fly on four. In simple terms, it is all to do with safety; if an engine fails in a 'twin', you are left with 50 per cent power, adequate to keep you in the air during flights over land, but not safe enough when there are long stretches of water. To test his aeronautical knowledge, I once asked a young student pilot who was learning to fly at Limerick why they fitted two engines in some aircraft, and he replied, 'So that if one engine fails, the pilot will have something to listen to before the crash.'

In the case of a four-engined design, loss of an engine

WHY DO THEY FIT TWO ENGINES ON SOME AIRCRAFT?
SO THAT IF ONE ENGINE FAILS, THE PILOT WILL HAVE SOMETHING TO LISTEN TO BEFORE THE CRASH.

leaves you with a comfortable 75 per cent of thrust which, even at maximum weight, is enough to ensure safe flights, whatever lies below the aircraft. In the bad old days, when we had to rely on piston engines, power failure was a part of everyday life, but the advent of the jet has brought with it standards of reliability that would have been considered quite impossible to attain not all that many years ago.

This improbable little drama was enacted half-way across the Atlantic. Outside is the blackest of nights with no moon and very few stars to be seen. Suddenly there is a loud bang and about twenty yards of flame stream from the rear of the outer engine on the left-hand side (known in the trade as No. 1 engine). The flame continues to burn for about fifteen seconds and then goes out. Then an Irish voice is heard over the cabin-announcement system, 'Ladies and gentlemen, this is your first officer speaking. As you may have noticed, we've had a little bother out there on the left-hand side, but we have three good engines flying us and we expect to arrive at Dublin about an hour late.'

All this is accepted with polite disinterest by the passengers, but some ten minutes later there is another loud bang followed by twenty yards of flame from the outer engine on the right-hand side (No. 4). As the fire goes out, the same voice announces, 'Ladies and gentlemen, this is your first officer again. We've had more trouble, this time on the right-hand side. But you are not to worry yourselves because we have two good engines up here and they will bring us into Dublin about two and a half hours late.'

Again the announcement is received without any outward signs of emotion until, some ten minutes later, there is another ear-shattering bang as a further twenty yards of flame shoot from the rear of the inner engine on the left (No. 2). By now the fare-paying inmates are beginning to engage themselves in some mildly animated conversation which ceases as 'the voice' says, 'Ladies and gentlemen, as you may have imagined, this is your first officer again. You might have noticed that we have had more trouble, again on the left of the aircraft, but we have a good engine fighting for us up here and we shall be arriving at Dublin about six hours late.'

Down at the back of the cabin, two young Irish chaps had been knocking off the beer and playing cards. To an outside observer the events of the past thirty minutes have made no impression whatsoever on these worthies. But that last announcement has run an alarm bell. 'Will you listen to dat,' said one to the other, 'if the last one goes, we'll be up 'ere all noite!'

And in conclusion

Actors often warn one another never to go on stage with children or animals because they tend to steal the show. Some of the true animal stories related to aviation are more astonishing than downright funny, but a friend of mine once landed a Viscount freighter at a German airport. There he was to pick up a baby elephant and fly it to a zoo in Britain. After filling in forms in the airport office, he walked back to the plane and there was a man in a white coat standing by a baby elephant. It was on some sort of a lead which looked like a thin length of string.

'What the hell is that?' exploded the captain. 'I expected it to be in a box. No way am I going to fly a loose elephant back to England.'

'No, please, I promise you it is just like a domestic dog and I shall be with it on the flight to make sure there is no trouble,' insisted the German keeper.

While all this was going on, Jumbo was standing there cross-eyed, gently removing car keys and loose change from the captain's pocket with its trunk and throwing them on to the tarmac with obvious pleasure.

Under some pressure, the captain reluctantly agreed to fly his unusual passenger and, sure enough, the little elephant clambered aboard the aircraft as though it had been flying all its life. During the take-off everything was fine. Throughout the climb Jumbo was a perfect gentleman. But during the cruise he started to march up and down the long cabin of the freighter while Mr Keeper fought a losing battle, trying to keep him in one place.

Now all this carry on was upsetting the balance of the aircraft. The autopilot gave up trying and went on strike and the two pilots up front spent the entire trip heaving their control wheels back and forth in an effort to maintain level flight.

It was while in the final stages of the flight that Jumbo decided he had just about enough of flying and registered his disapproval by having a leak on the floor. Of course, the two pilots were oblivious of what was going on until, on the final approach to land, full flap was lowered, the nose of the aircraft went down about five degrees and several gallons of Jumbo's relief trickled under the flight-deck door. I am told the capacity of a baby elephant is quite remarkable.

Well, that just about wraps up all I have to say. One or two readers of a literary inclination might consider the plot in this little book to be a bit thin, but I excuse myself on the grounds that I have made it all up as my fingers pounded this steaming, red hot computer. As an ancient pilot, I have naturally concentrated on aviation as seen from the flight-deck, but all branches of aeronautics have their tales to tell. Yes indeed, the serious business of flying has its funny side.

MY
OTHER
PLANE
IS A
747